IMAGES of NATURE

A JOURNEY THROUGH BRITAIN'S INSPIRATIONAL LANDSCAPES

IMAGES *of* NATURE

ADRIAN MUNSEY

Photographs by Adrian Munsey
except where separately credited

Text by Adrian Munsey

Gazetteer written by Hilary Brown

Designed by Chris Green *at* Colors
Artwork by Phil Berry
Photo of Adrian Munsey by Chris Green
Indexing by Ann Parry

Printed by The Printing House, Chester
Published in 2014 by Odyssey

ISBN 978-0-9555871-1-5

To my wife, Julia, and three children – Katherine, Imogen and Hugo –
who have put up with my various obsessions.

Contents

Acknowledgements

I have talked to many people in the development of this book and I gratefully acknowledge the help of Raymond Williams, Edmund Leach, John Dixon Hunt, Noel Machin, Michael Dames and Kenneth Jackson.

The quotations in the Celtic section are all taken from the Penguin edition of *Celtic Miscellany*, translated and edited by Kenneth Jackson. The quotations in the Medieval section from *Sir Gawain and the Green Knight* are all taken from the Penguin edition, translated and edited by Brian Stone.

The Department of Photography, Film and Television at the London College of Printing and the late George Lewinski helped me develop the photographic material and the book packager Bellew & Higton took the 1979 book to the Frankfurt Book Fair. Ib Bellew and Bernard Higton were very helpful in developing my ideas of how the book might look.

Subsequently, in 2014, designer Chris Green has finally and patiently turned this long gestation into the book that is now complete.

I also owe a debt to my car, a 1972 Lancia Fulvia Zagato S2, in which I travelled throughout the British Isles. This car was a great support to me, and my interest in driving it took me to more locations than perhaps a more ordinary car would have led me.

MISTS MERGED DAMPLY WITH THE MOORS

FROM SIR GAWAIN AND THE GREEN KNIGHT

Preface

This is a book that was started in 1976. I had intended *Images of Nature* to be an academic book, illustrated with paintings, architecture and my own photographs. I consulted many writers and historians. It was intended to be a film as well. I had an exhibition at the Felicity Samuel Gallery of photographs and projections based on the images.

I travelled in the mid 1970s throughout the British Isles. I looked at countless landscapes. Sometimes everything seemed 'natural' and the cultural distinctions being made did not always mean a lot. I wanted to explore the conflict between the idea of continuity and the idea of cultural change. I also wanted to look at anthropological, psychological and synchronic concepts.

I initially saw landscape as capable of being seen as both cultural and personal sets of codes and feelings. Structural ideas then seemed to offer a more abstract base for these forms of analysis. Food, shelter and sex – the codes all seemed to be to do with these structural functions.

Now in 2014, I have put the elements back together. There is a narrative and my photographic images are set against the quotations of poetry and philosophy about nature that always moved me.

What I always liked doing was just looking at landscapes. The framing of them gave me a sense of participation and the hope of a more permanent relationship with what I felt. The idea of being put in contact with something that was lost to me through looking at landscapes was very real. Looking meant feeling more in touch, though it was often only for moments or at best minutes.

Adrian Munsey

NATURE IS IN THE INSIDE

Introduction

The images man has had of nature have varied from seeing it as evil to seeing it as sublime. At times nature has been regarded as a mechanical clock, at other times as the soul of man itself. To early men and women, water tumbling down craggy rocks meant not so much a pretty scene to paint or photograph as danger – the danger which nature presents when man is not protected by firearms and waterproof clothing. The writer of *Beowulf* wrote:

They possess unknown land, wolf-cliffs, windy crags, a dangerous fen path, where the mountain stream falls down under the darkness of the rocks, a flood under the earth…over it hang lime-covered groves; the wood firm-rooted overshadows the water…that is an eerie place when the wind stirs up hostile storms till the air darkens, the skies weep. THE SONG OF BEOWULF

Landscape art and poetry have changing perceptions of nature and landscape. Often the same piece of land is depicted in entirely different ways. In the case of landscape gardening, the land itself is actually transformed according to the dominant view of nature, and this transformation may have many forms.

Between 1975 and 1979 I travelled throughout the British Isles taking photographs for this book. The form I decided on was extracts from key poems and philosophy – an anthology of what evoked meanings for their time and for me – combined with my photographs. It starts with prehistoric man and ends with the present day and explores seven of the most defined attitudes – Prehistoric, Celtic, Medieval, Pastoral, the Landscape Garden, Romanticism and Twentieth Century. It is not intended to be complete or comprehensive.

Adrian Munsey

CONSTABLE SAW STONEHENGE AS A WILD SET OF STONES,
HARDY AS AN ALTAR ON WHICH TESS LAY

I SHALL CONCLUDE WITH THE STONES CALLED THE GREY WETHERS, WHICH LYE SCATTERED ALL OVER THE DOWNES ABOUT MARLEBOROUGH, AND INCUMBER THE GROUND FOR AT LEAST SEVEN MILES DIAMETER; AND IN MANY PLACES THEY ARE, AS IT WERE, SOWN SO THICK THAT TRAVELLERS IN THE TWYLIGHT AT A DISTANCE TAKE THEM TO BE FLOCKS OF SHEEP (WETHERS) FROM WHENCE THEY HAVE THEIR NAME. SO THAT THIS TRACT OF GROUND LOOKS AS IF IT HAD BEEN THE SCENE WHERE THE GIANTS HAD FOUGHT WITH HUGE STONES AGAINST THE GODS, AS IS DESCRIBED BY HESIOD IN HIS THEOGONIA.

THE NATURAL HISTORY OF WILTSHIRE - JOHN AUBREY

In 1648 John Aubrey, riding through Avebury, was the first person of his age to notice it. He thought it was a prehistoric temple. *'Sir Christopher Wren says "they doe pitch all one way, like arrowes shot". Causere de hoc, and if so to what part of the heavens they point? Sir Christopher Wren thinks they were cast up by a volcano.'* THE NATURAL HISTORY OF WILTSHIRE - JOHN AUBREY

The inhabitants of the village of Avebury had thought it was evil, and had set about systematically destroying the monument. Neolithic monuments have had many and various meanings ascribed to them. Each age ascribes to them its own view of nature. Constable saw Stonehenge as a wild set of stones, Thomas Hardy as an altar on which Tess lay. Modern commentators like Alexander Thom and John Michell, as well as Sir Christopher Wren, suggest it was both an observatory and a centre of earth fields or soul currents – literal forces of nature centred on prehistoric monuments.

Certainly the idea of the British landscape being traversed by intersecting ley lines that seem to evoke the acupuncture or chakra points of the human body is immensely attractive as a vision of a landscape-based world that is complete and rather magical.

Claude Lévi-Strauss may not exaggerate when he finds in the Neolithic: *'a consuming symbolic ambition such as humanity has never again seen rivalled, and by scrupulous attention directed entirely towards the concrete, and finally by the implicit conviction that these two attitudes are but one.'* THE SAVAGE MIND - CLAUDE LÉVI-STRAUSS

Conventional archaeologists regard the monuments as temples or fortresses. All will admit that they have extraordinary design and atmosphere.

Whatever later ages have thought of prehistoric man, and whatever the scale of contemporary disagreements, some things can be said of how prehistoric man regarded nature.

Prehistoric man seems not to have differentiated himself from nature. He was part of it, part of the cosmos. He was born out of the earth, and buried in the earth. When I stand in prehistoric sites now, this is certainly what I feel.

PREHISTORIC MAN WAS BORN OUT OF THE EARTH,
AND BURIED IN THE EARTH

The White Horse is, I believe, by far the earliest hill drawing we have in England. It is a piece of design, also, in another category from the rest of the great chalk figures, for it has the lineaments of a work of art. The horse, which is more of a dragon than a horse, is cut from the top of the down's crest, so that it is only seen complete from the air or, at a long view, from the surrounding country. Seen on its own hill, it becomes an affair of violent foreshortenings or tapering perspectives more or less indecipherable. But, it was precisely this aspect of the Horse design that I found so significant. Once the rather futile game of 'picking out' the White Horse is abandoned, the documentary importance of the site fades, and the landscape asserts itself with all the force of its triumphant fusion of natural and artificial design. You then perceive a landscape of terrific animation whose bleak character and stark expression accord perfectly with its lonely situation on the summit of the bare downs. OUTLINE - PAUL NASH

Nature and culture could therefore be said to be one. It is an urban society that creates the distinction between them. Prehistoric man worshipped the nature deity. The movement of the stars and the progress of the seasons were of vital interest to him. Prehistoric science and its surprisingly effective technology were in harmony with nature and in accordance with it.

The prehistoric world sometimes seems a magic place. Also cold and harsh, though there is evidence that climatic conditions have greatly altered since Neolithic times.

A sense of the human soul and of fertility grew out of the worship of nature. As the American Indians who met the Swiss psychologist C. G. Jung felt, it is as if nature had to be helped by man to allow the processes of growth and renewal to occur.

In the pagan mystery religions, ceremony played a central part. In the present-day Lammas festivals, harvest suppers, hobby horses and other folk activities, this mystery religion lingers on.

The preoccupation of the stones has always been a separate pursuit and interest aside from that of object-personages. My interest began with the discovery of the Avebury megaliths when I was staying at Marlborough in the summer of 1933. The great stones were then in their wild state, so to speak. Some were half-covered by the grass, others stood up in the cornfields were entangled and over-grown in the copses, some were buried under the turf. But they were always wonderful and disquieting, and, as I saw them then, I shall always remember them... Their colouring and pattern, their patina of golden lichen, all enhanced their strange forms and mystical significance. Thereafter, I hunted stones, by the seashore, on the downs, in the furrows. LANDSCAPE OF THE MEGALITHS - PAUL NASH

In virtually all pre-Christian societies the basis of the mystery religions was nature worship. Soul and fertility both arose out of the worship of nature. In ceremonies still enacted in Britain today the remnants of these religions remain. Christianity adopted many components of these Orphic-like mysteries.

A LANDSCAPE OF TERRIFIC ANIMATION Outline - Paul Nash

THEIR COLOURING AND PATTERN, THEIR PATINA
OF GOLDEN LICHEN, ALL ENHANCED THEIR
STRANGE FORMS AND MYSTICAL SIGNIFICANCE.
THEREAFTER, I HUNTED STONES, BY THE
SEASHORE, ON THE DOWNS, IN THE FURROWS.

LANDSCAPE OF THE MEGALITHS – PAUL NASH

THEY DOE PITCH ALL ONE WAY, LIKE ARROWES SHOT

Sir Christopher Wren, quoted in The Natural History of Wiltshire - John Aubrey

A CONSUMING SYMBOLIC AMBITION SUCH AS HUMANITY HAS NEVER AGAIN
SEEN RIVALLED, AND BY SCRUPULOUS ATTENTION DIRECTED ENTIRELY
TOWARDS THE CONCRETE, AND FINALLY BY THE IMPLICIT CONVICTION
THAT THESE TWO ATTITUDES ARE BUT ONE.

CLAUDE LÉVI-STRAUSS ON THE NEOLITHIC IN THE SAVAGE MIND

Gazetteer

CALLANISH, Isle of Lewis, Outer Hebrides
A stone circle aligned with the landscape

With their precise placing in a wild and beautiful lake-strewn expanse, the Callanish Stones are a striking example of prehistoric man's ability to align landscape sculpture with his surroundings.

Dating from around 2900–2600 BC and laid out in the rough shape of a Celtic cross, the Stones consist of a primary circle some 13 metres in diameter approached by a long processional avenue from the north with shorter stone avenues to the south, west and east. Made from local gneiss rock, they average some 4 metres in height.

Local legends abound about the Stones – that they were giants who were petrified for refusing to convert to Christianity – and there has been much speculation about their devotional purpose, including the possibility that they were a 'stone calendar' aligned with the position of the moon.

CASTLERIGG STONE CIRCLE, Cumbria
The Lake District's striking prehistoric landmark

The Castlerigg Stone Circle near Keswick in the Lake

District is one of the most visually impressive in Britain. Set in a natural amphitheatre in this striking stretch of the Lake District, the stones look out on some of Cumbria's highest peaks, including Helvellyn, Skiddaw, Grasmoor and Blencathra. One of the country's oldest stone circles (probably dating from 3200 BC), Castlerigg provides further evidence of prehistoric man's ability to position such structures in evocative settings.

Many proposals have been made for Castlerigg's precise purpose. Some believe it may have been a mourning site for funeral rites, or a meeting place for traders. Some of the stones also appear to have been aligned with surrounding landscape features to mark the midwinter sunrise and various positions and phases of the moon.

RING OF BRODGAR, Orkney
The heart of Neolithic Orkney

The stone circle and henge of the Ring of Brodgar is the most northerly circle henge in the British Isles and is the finest known truly circular late Neolithic or early Bronze Age stone ring. Standing on a small isthmus between Stenness and Harray lochs on the main island of Orkney, the Ring of Brodgar is also one of the largest stone circles, and has World Heritage status along with several other adjacent Neolithic sites on Orkney, including Skara Brae and the Standing Stones of Stenness. It probably dates from 2500–2000 BC.

Such sites stand as a visible symbol of the achievements of prehistoric peoples far removed from other major contemporaneous civilisations and proclaim the triumph of the human spirit in early ages and isolated places.

SKARA BRAE, Orkney
Europe's most complete Neolithic village

On the far, curving shore of the bay lies Skara Brae, hazy through the sea-haar – George Mackay Brown –

In 1850, a great storm battered the Orkney Isles. The extreme wind and exceptionally high tides stripped the grass from a large mound known as 'Skerrabra' in the west mainland parish of Sandwick. But this storm damage served an unexpectedly positive purpose: it revealed one of the most remarkable ancient monuments in Europe.

Now known as Skara Brae, this World Heritage Site has been dubbed 'the British Pompeii'. It was occupied from around 3100–2500 BC, consists of several stone houses linked by passageways, and is Europe's most complete Neolithic village.

The stripping of the grass exposed the outlines of a number of stone buildings, and the local laird, William Watt of Skaill, was sufficiently intrigued to start excavations. By 1868, four houses had been revealed before Watt abandoned his excavations. Further work by the distinguished archaeologist Vere Gordon Childe during 1927–30 repaired the damaged structures and revealed new ones – for the first time the full extent of this stunning archaeological discovery became known.

Thanks to the sand that had covered the settlement for some 4,000 years, both the buildings and their contents were in a remarkable state of preservation, offering an unparalleled glimpse into how Neolithic man lived in this windswept landscape close to the sea.

Each house shares the same basic design: a large square room with a central fireplace, a bed to each side, and a shelved dresser on the wall opposite the doorway. The houses also contain a number of stone-built pieces of furniture, including cupboards, seats and storage boxes – there was even a primitive form of lavatory in each dwelling linked to a surprisingly sophisticated drainage system. Archaeologists believe that these structures were originally roofed with whalebone, timber and thatch.

So were the inhabitants of Skara Brae farmers living a simple pastoral life or were they some kind of mystical ruling elite? This remains a point of debate, but it has been established that a Neolithic 'low road' connects Skara Brae to the nearby ceremonial sites of the Maeshowe tomb chamber, the Standing Stones of Stenness and the Ring of Brodgar.

SILBURY HILL, Wiltshire
The largest prehistoric man-made mound in Europe

Of all the archaeological enigmas that comprise the Avebury prehistoric complex, Silbury Hill is the most intriguing. Amid a landscape rich in stone circles, burial chambers and hill-forts, in sheer terms of scale and engineering it is also the most striking example of prehistoric man's ability to transform the landscape into his own creation. In terms of height and volume, it rivals some of Egypt's pyramids.

Silbury's breast-like, man-made mound rises out of the Wiltshire plain just south-west of the Avebury Stone Circle. Some 40 metres high, 160 metres wide and dating from 2400 BC, it was built up over a period of time and according to legend is the last resting place of King Sil (or Zel) and his golden horse.

A monument to immense technical skill and well-organised human labour (it took some four million man-hours to build),

Silbury Hill's purpose remains teasingly obscure, despite numerous archaeological excavations. The first was recorded by the seventeenth-century antiquarian John Aubrey in 1680–82, and in 1776 a shaft was sunk vertically from the hill's flat summit in an attempt to uncover Sil's burial chamber and its supposed horde of gold. It yielded nothing, as did a shaft dug horizontally in 1849 from the hill's edge to the centre.

These and subsequent excavations may have revealed much about the hill's structure, but little about its purpose. In 2002, the 1776 excavations collapsed and a 14-metre-deep crater appeared in the hill's summit, requiring a major stabilisation project. But in 2007 an exciting 'find' was confirmed: evidence of a significant Roman settlement at the base of the hill.

Right up to the present, Silbury Hill has refused to yield up its secrets. Although the hill itself cannot be accessed, it can be viewed from nearby.

STONEHENGE, Wiltshire
The world's most famous and mysterious stone circle

Stonehenge

*Pile of Stone-henge! So proud to hint yet keep
Thy secrets, thou lov'st to stand and hear
The plain resounding to the whirlwind's sweep
Inmate of lonesome Nature's endless year.*
— WILLIAM WORDSWORTH

Stonehenge needs no introduction. A UNESCO World Heritage Site since 1986, it is probably the most famous prehistoric stone circle in the world, a place of pilgrimage for tourists and neo-Druids alike.

Its popularity has detracted from its impact. Nineteenth-century depictions of Stonehenge by landscape artists such as John Constable and J. M. W. Turner show the monument still standing in splendid isolation amid the vast, bleak expanses of Salisbury Plain, disturbed by nothing more than a flight of birds, a flock of sheep and inclement weather. In the words quoted above, the poet William Wordsworth responded to Stonehenge's 'sublime' quality, remoteness and inherent mystery, and Thomas Hardy captured the desolate spirit of the stones in one of his most famous passages from *Tess of the d'Urbervilles*. Now visitors from all over the globe arrive by the coach-load, and the traffic on the A303 thunders past with alarming proximity.

But Stonehenge nevertheless remains a powerful symbol of this country's ancient past and an astounding demonstration of the skill and ingenuity of those who built it – some of the circle's massive, four-tonne stones were transported by land and water all the way from the mountains of South Wales.

Both its age and purpose are moot points, but the common consensus is that it was constructed in three phases over a period dating from 3000 to 1600 BC and may have been a place for sun-worship and human sacrifice, a healing sanctuary or a sacred burial site.

Interest in ancient sites such as Stonehenge dates back to the seventeenth century and the pioneering work of antiquaries and archaeologists such as John Aubrey, John Evelyn and William Stukeley.

Wiltshire contains the greatest concentration of the Neolithic and Bronze Age monuments, and Stonehenge is believed to be part of an extensive network of sacred sites and burial mounds, including the nearby Silbury Hill and stone circle complex at Avebury.

VALE OF THE WHITE HORSE, Berkshire/Oxfordshire
A mythical dragon and an ancient, man-made horse

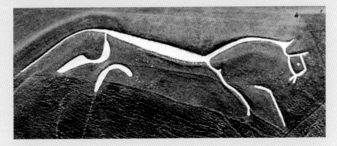

In the 1930s, John Betjeman lived in the little village of Uffington, which lies at the foot of the rolling Berkshire Downs, close to Faringdon and Wantage. From there, he could look a mile or two south and perhaps just make out a trio of ancient and mystical landscape features: Uffington Castle, the White Horse and Dragon Hill. All three overlook the beautiful stretch of countryside known as the Vale of the White Horse and lie just below that prehistoric thoroughfare the Ridgeway, which runs along the crest of the escarpment.

Is the flat-topped, naturally occurring conical mound of Dragon Hill, which nestles in the fold of the Downs, really where St. George slew the mythical beast? So legend has it, the dragon's blood spilling onto the summit and leaving a bare patch where no grass will grow. And does the peculiarly stylised White Horse, the massive figure carved by man into the chalk of the hillside, really descend on moonlit nights into the strange valley known as the Manger to graze?

As with other hill figures, such as the Cerne Giant, the White Horse's full impact can only be appreciated from the air. But in no way does this detract from the atmosphere of this windswept landscape, which has been the subject of myth and folklore for over 1,000 years.

Some 110 metres long, the White Horse is by far the oldest of the equine hill-figures that dot the landscape of southern England, and recent research has dated the figure to between 1400 and 600 BC. It may represent a horse-goddess (possibly Epona) worshipped by the local Bronze Age tribe, or may be some other tribal symbol associated with the original builders of the adjacent hill-fort of Uffington Castle. Its distinctive image still resonates in modern popular culture, from Terry Pratchett's *Discworld* books and Kate Bush videos to album covers by XTC and Nirvana.

Uffington Castle has similarly ancient origins. Excavations indicate that it was probably first built in the 8th or 7th century BC and was developed to an impressive scale during the Iron Age before being colonised by the Romans.

WAYLAND'S SMITHY, Oxfordshire
An ancient tomb chamber linked to a pagan god

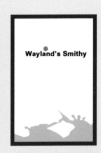

Legend has it that this impressive long barrow and tomb chamber, sited high on the Berkshire Downs on the ancient thoroughfare of the Ridgeway, is the burial place of Wayland (or Wolund), the Norse and Saxon god of blacksmithing. Visited at dusk or under a lowering sky on a winter's day, Wayland's Smithy retains a powerful aura of myth and magic: legend also has it that a traveller whose horse has cast a shoe can leave his mount and a silver coin on the burial chamber's capstone at nightfall and return the following morning to find his horse shod and the silver coin nowhere in sight.

Excavations carried out on this Neolithic site in the 1960s revealed that it was constructed in two phases: a timber structure dating from around 3700 BC superseded by a stone structure of c. 3400 BC. The tomb chamber is cruciform and archaeologists have uncovered evidence of several burials.

Close by along the Ridgeway are two other great prehistoric monuments: the Uffington White Horse and Uffington Castle, both overlooking the ancient Vale of the White Horse.

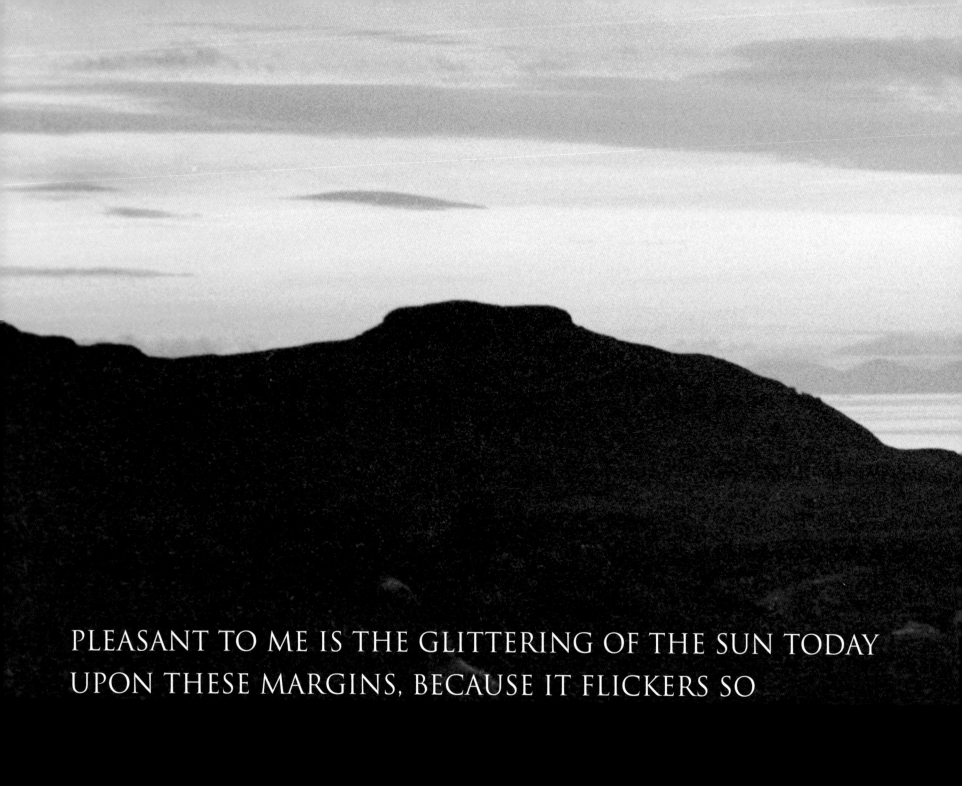

PLEASANT TO ME IS THE GLITTERING OF THE SUN TODAY
UPON THESE MARGINS, BECAUSE IT FLICKERS SO

Images of Nature | CELTIC

Pleasant to me is the glittering of the sun today upon these margins, because it flickers so. Irish, C9 - from Celtic Miscellany ed. Kenneth Jackson

The Celtic nature poetry of the seventh to the twelfth centuries was written in an aristocratic, feudal, sheltered society. Nature was not seen as the threatening force as portrayed in the Anglo-Saxon *Beowulf.*

The Celtic poets were protected from nature. The concept of a benevolent, attractive nature usually seems to be created by city-dwellers or the inhabitants of settled, non-agricultural courts and castles.

The Celtic societies of the fifth to the twelfth centuries created a courtly culture on the margins of the British Isles. These societies were based on earlier ones going back over a thousand years before Christ.

Poetry and decorative work were the major cultural creations of the Celtic artists. Celtic crosses and the abstract carving on them referring to landscape are widely known. Still virtually unknown is the poetry created by Celtic poets, much of it nature poetry expressing an overwhelmingly vivid relationship with the natural world.

No other culture, not even nineteenth-century Romanticism, is so powerfully able to evoke the experience of a transcendental world set in the distant landscapes of the western seas and isles.

There is an island far away, around which the sea-horses glisten, flowing on their white course against its shining shore; four pillars support it.

Colours of every hue gleam through the soft familiar fields; ranged around the music, they are joyful in the plain south of Argadnel.

Loveliness of a wondrous land; whose aspects are beautiful, whose view is fair, excellent, without a trace of mist …

Listening to music in the night, and going to Ildathach the many coloured land, a brilliance with clear splendour from which the white cloud glistens.

from Celtic Miscellany ed. Kenneth Jackson - Anon

Celtic nature poetry has an intense preoccupation with the beauty of nature. Imagination and freshness combine into short poems of transcendental power. They are the creation of the western edges of civilisation; it is as if heaven and earth are joined in imaginative unity.

As the poets lived in an aristocratic courtly society, this settled, sheltered environment, at least in the sense of protection from the elements, encouraged a vivid closeness with nature. So too does the actual look of the land itself.

In this archetypal landscape basic elements of land are framed by poetic enclosure into landscape vignettes. The lines of the poems seem to be powered by light. Sound and sense combine. Image and word are unified in an original way. There is an abiding sense of another world, which in some of the landscapes of the west coast of Scotland and Ireland seems to become reality.

He went to come out of the water then. "Do not come out," said Ailill, "till you bring me a branch of that mountain-ash on the bank of the river. Beautiful I think its berries". He went away and then broke a spray from the tree, and carried it on his back through the water...

And this is what Findabhair used to say afterwards of any beautiful thing which she saw, that she thought it more beautiful to see Froech across the dark pool; the body so white and the hair so lovely, the face so shapely, the eye so blue, and he a tender youth without fault or blemish, with face narrow below and broad above, and he straight and spotless, and the branch with red berries between the throat and the white face... FROECH IN THE DARK POOL IRISH, C8 - FROM CELTIC MISCELLANY ED. KENNETH JACKSON

There is no written work of any kind until the eighth century, but all Celtic poets seem to share an ability to see in full sensuous clarity.

Glen of fruit and fish and pools, its peaked hills of loveliest wheat, it is distressful for me to think of it – glen of bees, of long-horned wild oxen.

FROM CELTIC MISCELLANY ED. KENNETH JACKSON - ANON

THERE IS AN ISLAND FAR AWAY, AROUND WHICH THE SEA-HORSES GLISTEN

FROM CELTIC MISCELLANY ED. KENNETH JACKSON - ANON

Glen of cuckoos and thrushes and blackbirds, precious is its cover to every fox; glen of wild garlic and watercress, of woods of shamrock and flowers, leafy and twisting-crested.

Sweet are the cries of the brown-backed dappled deer under the oak-wood above the bare hill-tops, gentle hinds that are timid lying hidden in the great-treed glen.

Glen of the rowans with scarlet berries, with fruit fit for every flock of birds; a slumbrous paradise for the badgers in their quiet burrows with their young.

Glen of the blue-eyed vigorous hawks, glen abounding in every harvest, glen of the ridged and pointed peaks, glen of blackberries and sloes and apples.

Glen of the sleek brown round-faced otters that are pleasant and active in fishing; many are the white-winged stately swans, and salmon breeding along the rocky brink.

Glen of the tangled branching yews, dewy glen with level lawn of kine; chalk-white starry sunny glen, glen of graceful pearl-like high-bred women.

<small>DEIRDRE REMEMBERS A SCOTTISH GLEN   IRISH, C14 ‒ FROM CELTIC MISCELLANY ED. KENNETH JACKSON</small>

Epic and love poetry are set in sun, in snow, in land, in water, in ice. Storms erupt; the seasons pass. Nature is not viewed as a landscape; it is not merely felt; it is. As settlement was bare and rudimentary, nature was experienced in overwhelming physical reality.

How happy are the wild birds, they can go where they will, now to the sea, now to the mountain, and come home without rebuke. <small>TRADITIONAL WELSH, C17 ‒ FROM CELTIC MISCELLANY ED. KENNETH JACKSON</small>

Matthew Arnold felt that the Celtic tradition was a more profound source for poetry than the one starting with the English Renaissance.

LOVELINESS OF A WONDROUS LAND WHOSE ASPECTS ARE BEAUTIFUL

FROM CELTIC MISCELLANY ED. KENNETH JACKSON - ANON

HOW HAPPY ARE THE WILD BIRDS, THEY CAN GO WHERE THEY WILL...

...TO THE SEA, TO THE MOUNTAIN, AND HOME WITHOUT REBUKE.

Traditional Welsh, C17 - from Celtic Miscellany ed. Kenneth Jackson

GLEN OF THE RIDGED
AND POINTED PEAKS

DEIRDRE REMEMBERS A SCOTTISH GLEN IRISH, C14 - FROM CELTIC MISCELLANY ED. KENNETH JACKSON

A SLUMBROUS PARADISE FOR THE BADGERS IN THEIR QUIET BURROWS

FROM CELTIC MISCELLANY ED. KENNETH JACKSON - ANON

MANY ARE THE
WHITE-WINGED STATELY SWANS,
AND SALMON BREEDING ALONG
THE ROCKY BRINK

FROM CELTIC MISCELLANY ED. KENNETH JACKSON - ANON

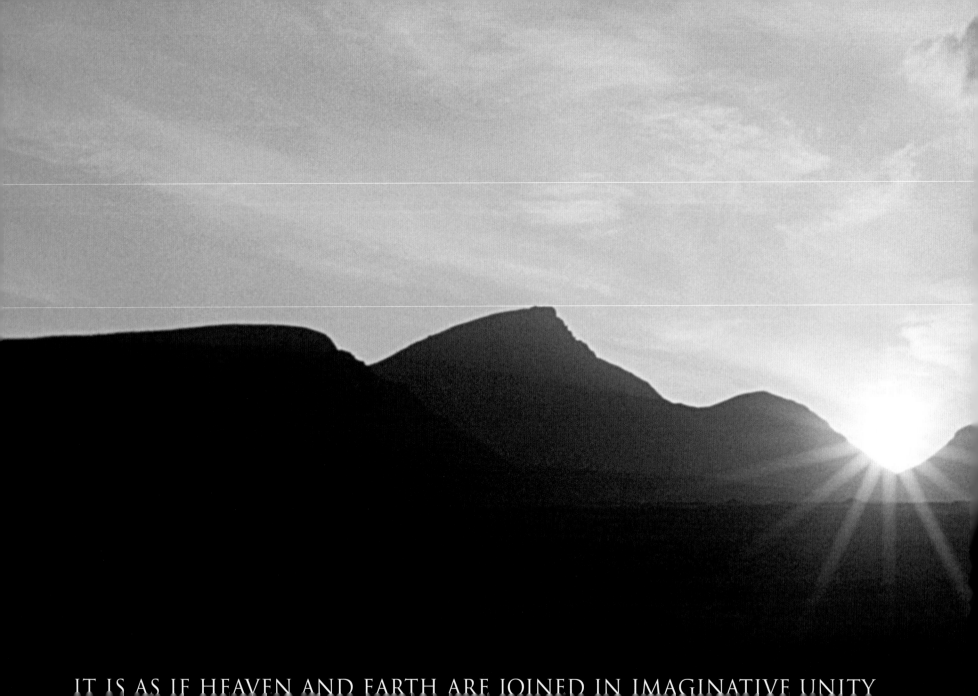

IT IS AS IF HEAVEN AND EARTH ARE JOINED IN IMAGINATIVE UNITY

THRICE THE SIGN OF THE SAVIOUR ON HIMSELF HE HAD MADE,
WHEN IN THE WOOD HE WAS AWARE OF A DWELLING WITH A MOAT
ON A PROMONTORY ABOVE A PLATEAU, PENNED IN BY THE BOUGHS
AND TREMENDOUS TRUNKS OF TREES, AND TRENCH ABOUT.
THE COMELIEST CASTLE EVER ACQUIRED BY A KNIGHT,
IT WAS PLACED IN AN IMPREGNABLE PALISADE OF POINTED STAKES,
ON A PLAIN WITH PARK ALL AROUND,
CONTAINING MANY TREES IN ITS TWO-MILE CIRCUMFERENCE...

SIR GAWAIN AND THE GREEN KNIGHT TR. BRIAN STONE

Images of Nature | **MEDIEVAL**

But wild was the weather the world awoke to;
Bitterly the clouds cast down cold on the earth.
Inflicting on the flesh flails from the north.
Bleakly, the snow blustered, and beasts were frozen;
The whistling wind wailed from the heights,
Driving great drifts deep in the dales.

SIR GAWAIN AND THE GREEN KNIGHT TR. BRIAN STONE

The general medieval view of nature seems to be that it was evil because mankind had been banished from the garden. Nature was therefore representative of man's fallen state.

Through this general view, however, an alternative view, perhaps based on Anglo-Saxon and Celtic literature combined with pagan remnants, burst through in the form of the Grail romances. Though many are influenced by French models, the greatest, *Sir Gawain and the Green Knight*, seems based on a north-western culture in Britain that disappeared with the English Renaissance.

The quest for the Grail is set in landscape. In England there are particular associations with West Wales, Glastonbury and Cadbury.

Thrice the sign of the Saviour on himself he had made,
When in the wood he was aware of a dwelling with a moat
On a promontory above a plateau, penned in by the boughs
And tremendous trunks of trees, and trench about.
The comeliest castle ever acquired by a knight,
It was placed in an impregnable palisade of pointed stakes,
on a plain with park all around,
Containing many trees in its two-mile circumference...

SIR GAWAIN AND THE GREEN KNIGHT TR. BRIAN STONE

In the two strands of the Grail legend we see an extraordinary parallel with the activities of artists working within the tradition of the transcendental landscape.

The Grail and the Green Man seemed to be saying that there is something essential that is natural and in communion with an external nature. Much later, the Romantic artists emphasising relationship with nature are not merely rebelling against the Enlightenment. They are reasserting the continuity of one of the great mysteries of life, which Jesse Weston calls 'the vegetative deity' or the 'nature myth'.

Without the restoration of the dead or dying king by the quester, the country becomes a 'Waste Land' and the crops die. On another, deeper level, the healing of the Fisher King introduces the quester into the mystery of life itself. The Christian religion after Hippolytus's destruction of the Mysteries betrays this continuous tradition of the myth of life, which goes back to earliest times.

The Grail appears to be both Christian symbol and pagan mystery. In its Christian form, the Grail is a cup or chalice from which Christ drank at the last supper. In its pagan form, the Grail is one of the great mysteries of life, containing within its nature the secrets of fertility and soul.

In the Grail romances, the two characteristics combine so that in its Christian form the quester for the Grail, after seeing it, passes at the moment of vision from the world 'and then sodenly his soule departed to Jhesu Christ, and a grete multitude of Angels bare his soule up to heven'.

In its pagan ritual form, we are told, it was 'not of wood, nor of any manner of metal, nor was it in any wise of stone, nor of horn, nor of bone, and therefore was he sore abashed'.

Scholars have associated the Grail with the widespread method in ancient times of symbolising the annual natural processes of growth and decay, of placing the animating spirit of nature in anthropomorphic form. The name of the god varied in different cultures. The earliest name is Tammuz, from Sumer and Babylonia, but the best known is that of the Greek god Adonis.

Dying a violent death, as the result of a chase of a wild boar, he descended to the netherworld, where he became the lover of the queen of Hades, Persephone. Aphrodite by passionate entreaty persuaded Zeus to restore her dead lover to life. Henceforth Adonis shares his existence between the upper and lower worlds. Each spring the return of Adonis was welcomed with popular rejoicing.

The myth of Adonis was taken up by the Naasenes, Christian mystics, who saw Christ as having similar attributes to Adonis. They were stigmatised by Hippolytus as heretics, and the continuity of this tradition of a spirit of nature in human form who died in order to be reborn through active intervention was lost to the formal Christian religion.

In the Grail romances, this myth lies beneath the Christian surface. In *Sir Gawain and the Green Knight* this theme is not directly treated, but it contains many of the myth's attributes.

Though this may seem rather esoteric, the significance lay in the representation of the soul and the opportunity to see it expressed in the forms of the natural world.

The Green Knight or Green Man is vital to certain fertility cults. Sir Gawain retains some of the attributes of a sun god or reborn fertility deity. The pagan material therefore consists of the sacrificed fertility god being resurrected and refertilising the waste land after winter.

THE COMELIEST CASTLE EVER ACQUIRED BY A KNIGHT

SIR GAWAIN AND THE GREEN KNIGHT TR. BRIAN STONE

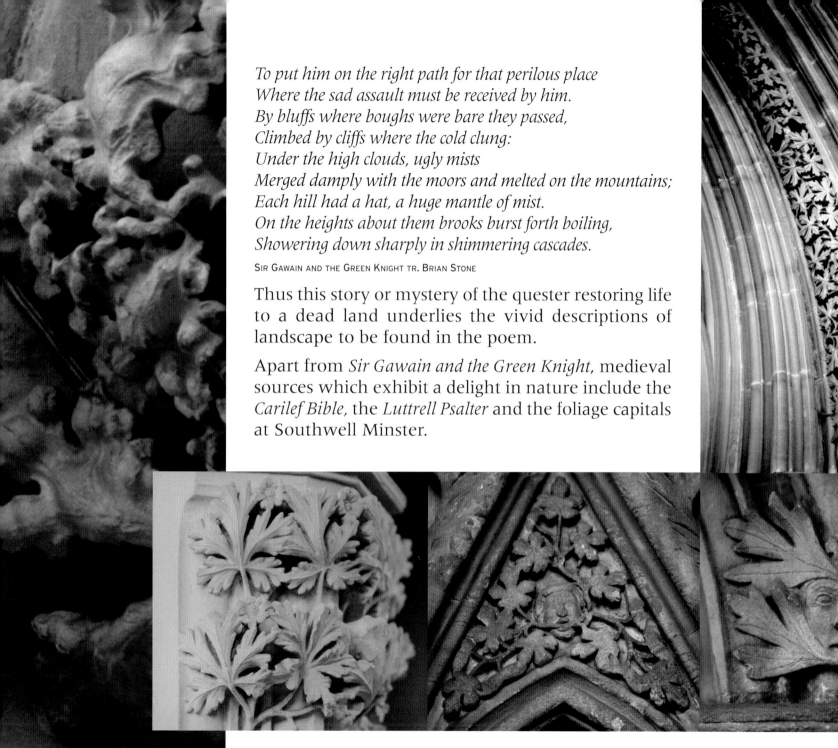

To put him on the right path for that perilous place
Where the sad assault must be received by him.
By bluffs where boughs were bare they passed,
Climbed by cliffs where the cold clung:
Under the high clouds, ugly mists
Merged damply with the moors and melted on the mountains;
Each hill had a hat, a huge mantle of mist.
On the heights about them brooks burst forth boiling,
Showering down sharply in shimmering cascades.

SIR GAWAIN AND THE GREEN KNIGHT TR. BRIAN STONE

Thus this story or mystery of the quester restoring life to a dead land underlies the vivid descriptions of landscape to be found in the poem.

Apart from *Sir Gawain and the Green Knight*, medieval sources which exhibit a delight in nature include the *Carilef Bible*, the *Luttrell Psalter* and the foliage capitals at Southwell Minster.

BY BLUFFS WHERE BOUGHS WERE BARE THEY PASSED,
CLIMBED BY CLIFFS WHERE THE COLD CLUNG

Sir Gawain and the Green Knight tr. Brian Stone

TO PUT HIM ON THE RIGHT PATH FOR THAT PERILOUS PLACE

Sir Gawain and the Green Knight tr. Brian Stone

ON THE HEIGHTS ABOUT THEM
BROOKS BURST FORTH BOILING,
SHOWERING DOWN SHARPLY IN
SHIMMERING CASCADES.

SIR GAWAIN AND THE GREEN KNIGHT TR. BRIAN STONE

CAERNARVON CASTLE, North Wales
A mighty symbol of conquest

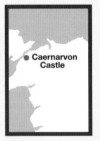

Caernarvon is one of the most imposing castles in Britain – and deliberately so. Its commanding, intimidating presence dominates the Menai Strait in North Wales. Caernarvon is, quite simply, the stamp of an invader's authority made in stone.

The castle was begun in 1283 by the English king, Edward I, following his conquest of the principality. His son, the first Prince of Wales (and later King Edward II), was born in the castle the following year. Although meant to emulate the dream castles of Welsh myth – 'the fairest that ever man saw' – the castle's design is decidedly masculine, and its sheer scale recalls the mighty imperial civic monuments of ancient Rome and the towering walls of Constantinople. Despite numerous attacks and sieges, the castle has survived remarkably intact and is now designated a World Heritage Site.

Prince Charles was formally invested with the title of 'Prince of Wales' at an elaborate ceremony held at the castle in 1969.

CAMELOT: THE ISLE OF AVALON and CADBURY, Somerset
The mystical landscape of King Arthur's Camelot

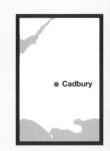

The Arthurian Legends have bred countless myths. But was King Arthur's Camelot an actual place or merely a powerful symbol of his universe?

Many British towns, cities, archaeological sites and landscapes have been proposed as the location of King Arthur's legendary castle and court, and the debate still rages. Chrétien de Troyes cites Caerleon in Wales in his 12th-century romance *Lancelot, the Knight of the Cart*.

In the 15th century, Thomas Mallory's epic poem *Le Morte d'Arthur* placed Camelot at Winchester. The capital of Wessex under King Alfred the Great, this ancient city was deemed a fitting location and it still boasts the relic known as the Winchester Round Table, said to be the legendary meeting place of Arthur and his Knights although it probably dates from the time of Henry VIII.

Other sites linked with Camelot include Colchester (on account of its Roman name of Camulodunum), and the dramatic castle ruins at Tintagel on the north Cornish coast.

By the mid 16th century, Cadbury Castle in Somerset was thought to be the original Camelot, and in the 1960s the site was extensively excavated in an effort to prove this supposition. No firm evidence was found, but in many minds the prehistoric hill-fort is still inextricably linked with the Camelot legend.

A nearby part of the Somerset Levels is often dubbed the legendary 'Isle of Avalon', and the town of Glastonbury that lies at its heart has been linked to the Arthurian Legends since the 12th century. The area certainly has a highly charged atmosphere, especially on days when the curious, conical Glastonbury Tor rises up out of a sea of low-lying mist.

Famed for its boisterous annual music festival, Glastonbury is also an epicentre for all things mystical – witness the New Age shops that cram the high street. Within the extensive abbey ruins lie the supposed graves of King Arthur and his queen, Guinevere. This claim has been dismissed as a publicity stunt staged by the abbey's monks to fund repairs after a disastrous fire, but the abbey remains a place of pilgrimage.

GLASTONBURY, Somerset
The setting for John Cowper Powys's sprawling mystic masterpiece

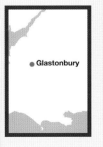

The novelist, poet and philosopher John Cowper Powys (1872–1963) has been called "one of the great puzzles of 20th century literature". His massive, sprawling novels – *A Glastonbury Romance, Wolf Solent, Weymouth Sands, Owen Glendower* and *Porius* being the most celebrated – greatly divide critics and readers, some regarding him as a literary god, others as a charlatan.

Powys had a strong affinity with the landscape, describing it in his books in meticulous detail and imbuing everyday places and objects with an almost psychic intensity. He loved walking and the open road and his intense sympathy with the whole of creation comes across strongly in his work – his godson described him as "dust and rock and feather and fin talking with a man's tongue".

Born in Derbyshire, Powys got to know many areas of Britain on his travels as an itinerant lecturer on English literature. He eventually settled in Wales, and Welsh myth and culture were powerful influences on his work.

Powys had a lifelong fascination with the Grail legend, and in *A Glastonbury Romance* (1932) he supplies a panoramic and highly individual portrait of this centre of New Age mysticism, its inhabitants and surrounding landscape.

FOUNTAINS ABBEY, North Yorkshire
A romantic medieval ruin meets the English Landscape Movement

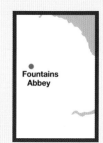

A UNESCO World Heritage Site (along with the adjacent Studley Royal Water Gardens), Fountains is one of the grandest and best-preserved abbey ruins in Britain.

As with nearby Rievaulx Abbey, Fountains was founded in 1132 on a site doubtless chosen for its sheltered location, complete with running water from the nearby River Skell and good local sources of timber and stone for building.

The original plan of the abbey adhered closely to the strict plans of the Cistercian order, but later alterations departed from this with the re-positioning of kitchens and guesthouses. Medieval monastic orders could be very adept at serving their own needs and creature comforts.

With Henry VIII's Dissolution of the Monasteries, Fountains Abbey was sold in 1540 to the London merchant Sir Richard Gresham and its order of monks disbanded. But even as the Abbey fell into ruin, it retained much of its romance, an aspect further enhanced in the 18th century with the intervention of the English Landscape Movement in the form of the spectacular Georgian water gardens.

SOUTHWELL MINSTER, Nottinghamshire
The mystery of the Green Man

Southwell
Minster

Nowhere in British ecclesiastical architecture is the enigmatic figure of the Green Man celebrated more exuberantly than in the world-famous 'Leaves of Southwell' in the chapter house of Southwell Minster, Nottinghamshire.

Look up the walls of the late 13th-century chapter house towards the vault (the only octagonal one in the country unsupported by a central pillar) and the eye becomes mesmerised by a riot of fabulous creatures both real and mythical, serpentine foliage, grimacing human heads, dragons playing hide-and-seek and the faces of ten 'Green Men' – part-human, part-nature, with leaves twisting out of their mouths. Such is the magnificence and quality of these carvings that Sir Nikolaus Pevsner was inspired to devote an entire book to them.

What is the significance of the Green Man? His origins are obscure and pagan, but he is primarily seen as a symbol of rebirth, fertility or good fortune. He crops up in many

cultures, and depictions of Green Men have occurred throughout history: from 2nd-century Roman columns in Turkey and Jain temples in Rajasthan to modern-day architecture in New York. In folklore and literature he may have links to the Nottinghamshire legend of Robin Hood and the epic poem *Sir Gawain and the Green Knight*.

Green Men have been part of mythology long before Christianity came to Britain, but this intriguing if rather eerie figure has been carved into the stone and wood of churches since the 11th century and in the Christian context may be representative of the risen Christ.

The visitor should take time to explore the Minster's other treasures. More Green Men can be found in the misericords of the 14th-century quire stalls and Charles Henry Simpson's quire pews (1886). The present Minster, which dates back to 1108 and gained cathedral status in 1884, boasts Roman remains, a fine Saxon tympanum carving showing St. Michael slaying the dragon, muscular Norman architecture, and a superb quire screen dating from 1337, its intricate stone fretwork boasting 286 heads of men, animals and grotesques and, in a touch of medieval mason's humour, a man scratching his bottom.

SWYTHAMLEY PARK and LUD'S CHURCH, Staffordshire
The legend of Sir Gawain and the Green Knight

Swythamley
Park

...a hillock of sorts, A smooth-surfaced barrow on a slope beside a stream...all hollow it was within, only an old cavern... – Sir Gawain and the Green Knight tr. Brian Stone

Tantalisingly, legend has long linked this area on the edge of the Peak District with the 14th-century Arthurian romance of *Sir Gawain and the Green Knight*. Local rumours abound of a headless rider appearing through the mist near Lud's Church, close to Swythamley Park – a figure said to be the Green Knight himself, that symbol of death, rebirth, chivalry and fertility decapitated by Sir Gawain at Camelot.

So did these two locations provide the poem's anonymous author with, respectively, the models for Sir Gawain's castle and the Knight's 'Green Chapel'? They certainly qualify in terms of 'greenness' alone, being a dankly atmospheric landscape of lush, winding valleys, ferny undergrowth and dripping trees.

Within the boundaries of Swythamley Park (which lies on the Staffordshire side of the River Thane between Leek and Buxton) stood the original Swythamley Hall, a medieval hunting lodge belonging to the nearby Abbey of Dieulacres (no longer extant), and it's possible that the poem's author had some sort of connection with the Abbey. The hall was granted to the Trafford family in 1540 by Henry VIII; it burnt down in 1813 and the current Swythamley Hall dates from that period.

Lud's Church – the putative 'Green Chapel' – is not, in fact, a church at all but a dramatic gritstone rock chasm extending into a hillside at Back Forest above Gradbach. It's possible that its name derives from Sir Walter de Lud Auk, leader of a group of medieval heretics who sought refuge in the chasm from religious bigots all too eager to burn them at the stake.

Certainly this damp, mossy, fern-covered enclosure would offer a perfect place of sanctuary, and legend has it that figures as diverse as Robin Hood and Bonnie Prince Charlie used it precisely for this purpose. Some 100 metres long and 18 wide, the chasm retains an air of cool mystery on even the hottest of days – it's said that the sun penetrates Lud's Church only on Midsummer Day.

Something less spectral but nearly as jolting as a headless horseman might surprise the visitor exploring this area: wild wallabies descended from those released from Swythamley Park's private zoo during the Second World War.

HERE AT THE FOUNTAIN'S SLIDING FOOT,

OR AT SOME FRUIT-TREE'S MOSSY ROOT,

CASTING THE BODY'S VEST ASIDE,

MY SOUL INTO THE BOUGHS DOES GLIDE:

THERE LIKE A BIRD IT SITS AND SINGS,

THEN WHETS AND COMBS ITS SILVER WINGS;

AND, TILL PREPARED FOR LONGER FLIGHT,

WAVES IN ITS PLUMES THE VARIOUS LIGHT

THE GARDEN - ANDREW MARVELL

Images of Nature | **PASTORAL**

It was during the late Middle Ages and Italian Renaissance that an interest in landscape started for its own sake. Painters began the trend. In England everything happened later, not in painting but in poetry. Dominating the pastoral form was the need to get away from 'real' nature. The garden, or controlled nature, was the main metaphor.

Nature becomes Arcadia – a magic land of the imagination requiring no labour for it to bear fruit. Sheep graze and courtiers become shepherds. More specially pastoral aesthetics authorised the first major enclosure movement, consequent social change and the depopulation of many villages. A concept of nature, a natural order of things, was being used to justify some very unpleasant, if not unnatural, happenings. This was to continue in landscape gardening, itself a product of pastoral attitudes.

There was a golden age – who murdered it?
How died that age, or what became of it?

FROM THE COLLECTED WORKS OF THOMAS MIDDLETON

Well was I, while under shade
Oaten Reedes me musicke made,
Striving with my mates in song,
Mixing mirth our songs among,
Greater was that shepherd's treasure,
Than this false, fine, courtly pleasure.

DISPRAYSE OF A COURTLY LIFE - SIR PHILIP SIDNEY

The pastoral theme is that man was born in a garden but was expelled from it. Ever since he has sought to return. The idea of a Golden Age is derived from Roman times.

They looking back, all th' eastern side beheld
Of Paradise, so late their happy seat,
Wav'd over by that flaming brand, the gate

With dreadful faces throng'd and fiery arms.
Some natural tears they dropped, but wiped them soon.
The world was all before them, where to choose
Their place of rest, and Providence their guide:
They, hand in hand, with wandering steps and slow,
Through Eden took their solitary way.

PARADISE LOST - JOHN MILTON

Theocritus and Virgil both wrote of an age of pastoral innocence when the entire world was seen as a garden. These writings became available again in Britain during the English Renaissance beginning in the early sixteenth century. The medieval garden of purely religious purpose was superseded by influences from Italy.

With the English Renaissance, the influence of Italy, and more settled life, poets turned to the pastoral form to express their love of land. Religion had become exceptionally controversial, and landscape was a readily available alternative. The pastoral form, in one sense mystifying the savage aspects of enclosure, was taken up by artists who were naive to its social accompaniment.

Walking in bright Phoebus' blaze
Where with heat oppreste I was,
I got to a shady wood,
Where greene leaves did newly bud.
And of grasse was plenty dwelling,
Deckt with pyde flowers sweetly smelling.

DISPRAYSE OF A COURTLY LIFE - SIR PHILIP SIDNEY

The countryside, created in imagination from the court, became an Eden of shepherds and flocks living in idealised, but in the poet's eyes more truthful, experience. It is hard now not to be suspicious of the pastoral impulse because of the ruthlessness employed to create the pastoral vision.

The range of pastoral experience derived from nature was limited in psychological intensity compared with the best that had gone before it, but wider in scope. A small paradise was created in these little gardens. They were not close to nature in our sense, but they were nevertheless very different from the medieval garden.

The actual gardens were greatly amplified in the writings of men such as Francis Bacon. All kinds of hermetic, alchemical and emblemic significance were attached to the paradise garden. Nature here was clearly not wild and untrammelled; it was limited, controlled and ideal.

A further development of this concept took place with pastoral poetry, where an Arcadian vision of a countryside needing no human labour was created.

From the late sixteenth century, the pastoral moves increasingly away from any real description of the country. It becomes more and more idealised, and is both the root of the mystification of the 'country' and, it can be argued, the source of all subsequent nature forms in poetry.

Turner and Constable in painting, just as Clare and Wordsworth in poetry, had to break through some of the atrophy of the pastoral form to put some real feeling into their work.

NUN APPLETON HOUSE, Yorkshire
Andrew Marvell and the art of the pastoral poem

Nun Appleton House

Here at the fountain's sliding foot,
Or at some fruit-tree's mossy root,
Casting the body's vest aside,
My soul into the boughs does glide:
There like a bird it sits and sings,
Then whets and combs its silver wings;
And, till prepared for longer flight,
Waves in its plumes the various light.

THE GARDEN – ANDREW MARVELL

Andrew Marvell (1621–78), metaphysical poet, Parliamentarian, friend and colleague of fellow poet John Milton, lived from 1650 to 1652 at Nun Appleton House near York as tutor to the daughter of Lord General Thomas Fairfax, former commander of Cromwell's army.

By then, Marvell had done much to foster his prodigious intellect: he had gone up to Trinity College, Cambridge at the age of 13, and had spent much of the Civil War years travelling on the Continent, expanding his education in such cultural centres as Rome and mastering several languages.

It was while living at this obscure country house that Marvell wrote some of his most memorable verse, including 'Upon Appleton House, To My Lord Fairfax', a meditation on war and political change, and what is probably his best-known poem, 'To His Coy Mistress'.

But it is 'The Garden' that, perhaps most significantly of all Marvell's poems, evokes the intellectual concept of 'the pastoral' and applies its ideas to the landscape immediately to hand – in this case the specific details and gentle features of the garden at Nun Appleton.

Using lush and sensual imagery, Marvell presents the garden as a tranquil and idyllic sanctuary where one might find temporary escape from the turbulent world of the Interregnum beyond the garden walls. Watching the bees going about their business, Marvell concludes the poem with the ecstatic lines:

And, as it works, th'industrious bee
Computes its time as well as we.
How could such sweet and wholesome hours
Be reckoned but with herbs and flowers!

THE GARDEN – ANDREW MARVELL

BORN TO GRACE NATURE, AND HER WORKS COMPLETE;
WITH ALL THAT'S BEAUTIFUL, SUBLIME AND GREAT!
FOR HIM EACH MUSE ENWREATHES THE LAUREL CROWN
AND CONSECRATES TO FAME IMMORTAL BROWN.

FROM THE RISE AND PROGRESS OF THE PRESENT TASTE IN PLANTING PARKS, PLEASURE GROUNDS, GARDENS, &C, FROM HENRY THE EIGHTH TO
KING GEORGE THE THIRD; IN A POETIC EPISTLE TO THE RIGHT HONORABLE CHARLES, LORD VISCOUNT IRWIN - ANONYMOUS

Images of Nature | **THE LANDSCAPE GARDEN**

The true history of the English countryside has been centred throughout in the problems of property in land, and in the consequent social and working relationship…it is only a short step from a natural delight in the fertility of the earth to (this) magical invocation of a land which needs no farming. The Country and the City - Raymond Williams

The garden is for many the paradigm for landscape. The history of the garden shows perhaps more clearly than any other art form how the images of nature that man has determine the form of the representation of landscape.

As a model for controlling nature, the landscape garden took up the convention built into the pastoral. The model is still with us in our own day and underlies most forms of planning, particularly experimental forms such as the new towns and garden cities.

Gardens were created as soon as settlements stabilised – around castles in the Middle Ages and in the growing number of country houses as soon as civil war became less frequent. In general, medieval man had disapproved of nature as it was reminiscent of man's fallen state.

The medieval gardens that did exist were emblematic of religion. Indeed, until 1700 nature was rarely perceived; it was conceived. Gardens were laid out as a set of religious emblems – or philosophical ideas. Man was clearly separate from nature.

Meanwhile the mind, from pleasures less,
withdraws into its own happiness:-
The mind, that ocean where each kind
Does straight its own resemblance find:-
Yet it creates, transcending these,
Far other worlds, and other seas,
Annihilating all that's made
To a green thought in a green shade. The Mower Against Gardens - Andrew Marvell

The sophistication of the seventeenth-century garden lent an edge to the charm of the uncultivated wilderness. Landscape gardening in the seventeenth century renewed itself as Puritan influences relaxed and allowed renewed contact with

Italy. The landscape architects were far behind the poets, but the beginnings of a change were occurring. Just the very fact of placing the house in a landscaped setting was important.

A garden such as Ham House was very influenced by Italy, and, in a very formal way, its wilderness began to show that the new attitudes to nature being pioneered by poets such as Milton and Marvell were beginning to have effect. Ham House is the only mid-seventeenth-century garden in existence, and exhibits all the features of influences from the Italian Renaissance and the faint beginnings of a less formal influence. In general, though, the French influence of Le Nôtre and the Dutch influence of topiary held sway.

By the late seventeenth century the Grand Tour was under way and new influences came to bear. The poet Marvell proved visionary of the change to come when he wrote in 1670:

Tis all enforced, the fountain and the grot,
While the sweet fields do lie forgot   THE MOWER AGAINST GARDENS - ANDREW MARVELL

It was 70 years before his words had effect. But the diarist Evelyn, the poet Pope and the essayist Addison all in the late seventeenth century began to argue for a more natural garden.

Our British gardeners instead of humouring Nature, love to deviate from it as much as possible. … I do not know whether I am singular in my opinion but, for my own part, I would rather look upon a tree in all its luxuriancy and diffusion, than when it is cut and trimmed into a Mathematical figure and cannot but fancy that an Orchard in flower looks infinitely more delightful than all the little labyrinths of the most finished parterre.

ADDISON IN SPECTAYTOR 1712

The greatest influences for change therefore came from Italy, from Claude's and Poussin's landscapes, and from Italian gardens. Renaissance Italy itself was influenced by Roman conceptions of nature as Arcadia. A counter influence came from France in the

form of neoclassical ideas, but the Italian influence prevailed. Whereas the French, who lived under tyranny, had tightly organised, restrictive gardens, the English, a 'free' people, had gardens in which they were at liberty to 'expiate freely'.

The great English supporters of a greater truth to nature were John Evelyn and Alexander Pope. The first change can clearly be seen at Levens Hall near Kendal in Cumbria.

The capital stroke, the leading step to all that has followed, was (I believe the first thought was Bridgeman's) the destruction of walls for boundaries, and the invention of fesses...At that moment appeared Kent...He leaped the fences, and saw that all nature was a garden.

LORD ORFORD'S WORKS VOLUME II P535

There Beaumont, gardener to James II and student of Le Nôtre, though laying out neoclassical designs and planting the great Dutch topiary garden, was instructed by the owner to build a ha-ha, and a park where trees followed the contours.

The influence of Addison and Pope meant that topographical artists and landscape gardeners sought to get closer to nature. Picturesque principles of setting prospects and views predominated, as well as walks within gardens and parks, where mental associations were created to stimulate the internal mental landscape of the walker.

It was this combination of the picturesque and mental association that underlies the beginnings of Romantic poetry. Wordsworth incidentally considered himself an authority on landscape gardening. Pope wrote:

All gardening is landscape painting – just like a landscape hung up…You may distance things by darkening and narrowing the plantation more and more towards the end, in the same manner as they do in paintings.

ESSAY ON GARDENS IN THE GUARDIAN (1713) - ALEXANDER POPE

TIS ALL ENFORCED, THE FOUNTAIN AND THE GROT,

...WHILE THE SWEET FIELDS DO LIE FORGOT

THE MOWER AGAINST GARDENS – ANDREW MARVELL

A WORK TO WONDER AT

Of Flowers And Flower Gardens - Alexander Pope

The clearest examples where it is possible to see now the picturesque principle of suggesting mental associations during walks are at Rousham, at Chiswick and in one part of Stowe designed by Kent.

The revolutionary technical development in the history of the landscape garden came with the invention of the ha-ha. Examples can be seen at Rousham and at Heaton Hall, Manchester. As William Kent proclaimed, 'Nature abhors a straight line' and he put this firmly into practice in his designs for Stowe.

The garden as picture reached its purest development at Stourhead. Picturesque principles here and at Stowe – of setting views and prospects – came to predominate.

Capability Brown, who must be the greatest of the gardeners, further evolved an ideal private world for the society he served. It was a world not of the work of a man, but seemingly of nature. Brown took up the ideas of the philosopher Burke, originator of the concept of the 'sublime'.

Most people have observed the sort of sense they have had of being swiftly drawn in an easy coach on a smooth turf, with gradual ascents and declivities. This will give a better idea of the Beautiful than almost anything else.

ON THE SUBLIME AND BEAUTIFUL - EDMUND BURKE

The final stages of the 'natural' garden revolution were therefore wrought by Capability Brown. In his landscaping each viewer was offered the opportunity for individual interpretation.

Curved lines and faithfulness to 'nature' dominated all his work. This style, imitated all over the world, was thus the work of one man:

Born to grace Nature, and her works complete;
With all that's beautiful, sublime and great!
For him each Muse enwreathes the Laurel Crown
And consecrates to Fame immortal Brown.

FROM THE RISE AND PROGRESS OF THE PRESENT TASTE IN PLANTING PARKS, PLEASURE GROUNDS, GARDENS, &C, FROM HENRY THE EIGHTH TO KING GEORGE THE THIRD; IN A POETIC EPISTLE TO THE RIGHT HONORABLE CHARLES, LORD VISCOUNT IRWIN - ANONYMOUS

ALL GARDENING IS LANDSCAPE PAINTING...

JUST LIKE A LANDSCAPE HUNG UP

Essay on Gardens in The Guardian (1713) - Alexander Pope

But there were other witnesses to the oppression of the landscape garden upon ordinary people.

There once were lanes in nature's freedom dropt,
There once were paths that every valley wound -
Inclosure came, and every path was stopt;
Each tyrant fix'd his sign where paths were found,
To hint a trespass now who cross'd the ground;
Justice is made to speak as they command;
The high road now must be each stinted bound:-
Inclosure, thou'rt a curse upon the land,
And tasteless was the wretch who thy existence plann'd...

O England! Boasted land of liberty,
With strangers still thou mayst thy title own,
But thy poor slaves the alteration see,
With many a loss to them the truth is known:
Like emigrating bird they freedoms flown,
While mongrel clowns, low as their rooting plough,

Disdain thy laws to put in force their own;
And every village owns its tyrants now,
And parish-slaves must live as parish kings allow

...Ye fields, ye scenes so dear to Lubin's eye,
Ye meadow-blooms, ye pasture-flowers, farewell!
Ye banish'd trees, ye make me deeply sigh,
Inclosure came, and all your glories fell.

FROM THE VILLAGE MINSTREL BY JOHN CLARE

Thomas Hardy was to sing a similar song of regret when mechanisation acted like enclosure in breaking up age-old patterns of existence of land. Framing of nature by fields restricted the range of relationship possible as did parks and classical landscapes. The poet had to take to the hills.

As in pastoral poetry, the socio-economic changes of the times are obscured by these changes. To build Capability Brown's parks, common lands were being enclosed and turned into sheep runs. Villagers were driven off the land to starve in the cities. The most extreme example of this was in the Sutherland clearances which are remembered to this day.

Nature had been completely transformed on the one hand by a man of genius, and on the other by a rentier society, which with its sheep runs enclosed and decimated the countryside, destroying common law rights and creating enormous suffering, and for over a hundred years forcing a permanent drop in working people's living standards. The ownership of land, always an index of wealth and status, was thus rendered invisible as a social and economic factor.

I grant indeed that fields and flocks have charms
For him that grazes or him that farms;
But when amid such pleasing scenes I trace
The poor laborious natives of the place,
And see the mid-day sun, with fervid ray,
On their bare heads and dewy temples play;
While some, with feebler heads and fainter hearts,
Deplore their fortune, yet sustain their parts;
Then shall I dare these real ills to hide
In tinsel trappings of poetic pride?

THE VILLAGE – GEORGE CRABBE

Gazetteer

HAMPTON COURT GARDENS, Middlesex
Palace gardens evolved over centuries

Cardinal Wolsey, Henry VIII, William III, Christopher Wren, Capability Brown – since Tudor times many great personalities have put their stamp on the grandiose royal palace of Hampton Court and its formal gardens south-west of London.

Nothing remains of the original Tudor gardens, but there is a 1920s re-creation of Henry VIII's knot garden of 1536. The parterre gardens and water features are largely contemporary with Christopher Wren's extensive building work during the 1690s and were doubtless influenced by such formal French gardens as those at Versailles.

Other features of the garden include the world-famous Maze, planted in the 1690s, and the Great Vine, planted by Capability Brown in 1768 and still producing a yearly crop of sweet, black grapes. Brown had been appointed Head Gardener at Hampton Court in 1764.

LEVENS HALL, Cumbria
A unique celebration of the art of topiary

The patient, meticulous clipping of evergreen shrubs and trees, such as yew or box, into fantastical shapes: such is the garden art of topiary, and nowhere is it celebrated more gloriously than at Levens Hall in Cumbria, regarded by many as the finest topiary garden in the world.

This ancient garden survives very much in its original form. It was laid out in 1694 by Guillaume Beaumont, who was said to be a pupil of Louis XIV's great gardener, Le Nôtre.

Topiary is considered to be a very British art, but it has been a garden feature since the time of the Romans.

The word itself derives from the Greek *topos*, or place, and the Latin word *topiarus* came to mean 'the man in charge of the place', or gardener. It was also a feature of Italian Renaissance gardens, but in this country its popularity has fluctuated.

The garden designer Vita Sackville-West disliked topiary that was too prettified, the 16th-century philosopher Francis Bacon considered it suitable only for the amusement of children, and the essayist Joseph Addison was positively scathing: "We see the mark of scissors upon every plant and bush... I would rather look upon a tree in all its luxuriancy and diffusion of boughs and branches".

ROUSHAM HOUSE GARDENS, Oxfordshire
William Kent's intimate masterpiece

'He leap'd the fence, and saw that all nature was a garden'. Nowhere are Horace Walpole's words about William Kent (1685–1748) more apposite than at Rousham, the landscape garden Kent created in the 1730s on a gentle curve of the River Cherwell some 10 miles north of Oxford.

The gardens of Rousham House are a delight – Kent's

pastoral and 'picturesque' celebration of a new Augustan age that recalled the glories and ethos of Ancient Rome. Designed on a sloping and partially wooded site, they are of major significance in the evolution of landscape gardening.

Not only are they one of the earliest examples of the more naturalistic and informal style that came into favour in the first half of the 18th century, they are also the only gardens by William Kent that survive virtually untouched since he created them nearly three centuries ago.

A perfect balance of art and nature, Rousham invites the visitor in with carefully planned 'surprises', winding woodland walks and ever-unfolding vistas.

Those strolling around the gardens today can enjoy many of the features that would have enchanted 18th-century visitors, including classical statuary, Venus' Vale, the Cold Bath, the serpentine rill, the seven-arched Praeneste, and the Gothic arch on the skyline known as the Eyecatcher.

Developing his garden from the foundations laid out by Charles Bridgeman, Kent took over the design of Rousham in 1737. Influenced by the landscape paintings of Poussin and Claude (indeed, Kent's friend the poet Alexander Pope stated that 'all gardening is landscape painting'), in essence Kent took the notion of a natural classical landscape and applied it to the English countryside: "the sweetest little groves, streams, glades, porticoes, cascades, and river, imaginable; all the scenes are perfectly classic," wrote Walpole of Kent's design.

Through the clever use of a ha-ha and rural views, Kent also ensured that his design 'extended' the garden into the surrounding landscape.

Rousham is a work of novelty and genius – 'the most engaging of all Kent's works', as Walpole put it. Little wonder that Walpole dubbed the polymath Kent, who also worked as an architect, painter, and furniture and stage-set designer, 'the father of modern gardening'.

STOURHEAD, Wiltshire
Henry Hoare's garden 'paradise'

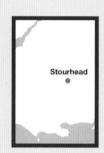

Stourhead

Inspired by painterly views of Italy, in the 1740s Henry Hoare II started to remodel the river valley that lay in the shadow of his Palladian mansion at Stourhead, Wiltshire. Hoare's landscape vision continued to evolve over the next 40 years and the result was one of the most significant, influential and beautiful gardens in the world. Indeed, Stourhead is so exceptional that it has been dubbed 'Paradise' and Hoare lauded as 'Henry the Magnificent'.

Stourhead is literally art brought to life – a perfect interpretation in the English countryside of classical landscapes by such artists as Claude, Poussin and Dughet, whose paintings men such as Henry Hoare would have seen while undertaking that obligatory experience for well-heeled 18th-century individuals: the Grand Tour of Europe. Various features also show the literary influence of the poet Alexander Pope.

Stourhead is a work of imaginative and inventive genius, and Hoare displayed great foresight and skill in creating its layout. As with William Kent's garden at Rousham, which likewise typifies the new informal style of the English landscape movement, the visitor is led through an ever-changing landscape of stunning views and surprise vistas.

Hoare dammed the River Stour, which rises at the head of the valley, to form a central 22-acre lake, around which he placed a selection of classical features, including the Temple of Flora, the noble Pantheon, the Temple of Apollo perched high on its hill, and the gothic delights of the Cottage and the Grotto.

The Grotto is a shadowy concoction of rusticated stone: Rysbrack's elegant sculpture of a nymph sleeps beyond a lively pool of water, and the floor bears the following lines from Pope:

Nymph of the grot, these sacred springs I keep
And to the murmurs of these waters sleep.
Ah, spare my slumbers, gently tread the cave
And drink in silence, or, in silence, lave.

Mr Pope's Literary Correspondence, Vol. 1, 1735

Hoare's landscape has been enriched with new planting, but Stourhead remains very much faithful to his brilliant original concept for the garden. Whatever the season or weather, Stourhead provides a spectacle that never ceases to astonish and delight the eye.

STOWE, Buckinghamshire
Capability Brown's training ground

Capability Brown, William Kent, John Vanbrugh, Charles Bridgeman, William Pitt, Jonathan Swift, William Congreve, Alexander Pope: many great figures from the worlds of garden design, politics and literature contributed in their own way to the creation of the magnificent 250-acre landscape garden at Stowe, "a work to wonder at".

Boasting numerous temples, monuments and statues, along with lakes and wooded valleys, Stowe's design developed the more informal style pioneered by the likes of Kent, Vanbrugh and Bridgeman in the early 18th century and was intended to score political points as well as to delight the visitor with its tranquil spaces and breathtaking views. It also provided an invaluable training ground for that 18th-century genius of the British landscape garden: Lancelot 'Capability' Brown (1716–83).

Stowe remained in the hands of the same family for some 350 years, and the garden as seen today evolved over many decades, but it was in the early part of the 18th century, under the influence of Lord Cobham and his nephew Richard Grenville, that the gardens were transformed from a modest French-style parterre into the resplendent showpiece the visitor enjoys today.

Cobham entertained his influential friends such as Congreve, Swift, Pope and the Prime Minister William Pitt at Stowe and incorporated their suggestions for making satirical sideswipes via various features in the garden.

As at Stourhead and Rousham, Stowe presented a sequence of ever-changing picturesque views to the visitor via a carefully planned perambulation. In the 1720s, Vanbrugh and Bridgeman designed an English baroque park, work that was expanded upon in the 1730s by Kent, who enclosed 40 acres to create the Elysian Fields and constructed two of the garden's most famous features: the Temple of British Worthies and the Temple of Ancient Virtue.

In 1742, the 26-year-old Capability Brown was appointed head gardener to work alongside Kent. Stowe thus effectively became Brown's first commission, and over the next decade he put his distinctive stamp on its landscape with his carefully planned but revolutionary 'naturalistic' remodelling of the lakes and parkland.

SO WAS IT WITH ME IN MY SOLITUDE;

SO OFTEN AMONG MULTITUDES OF MEN.

UNKNOWN, UNTHOUGHT OF, YET WAS I MOST RICH -

I HAD A WORLD ABOUT ME - 'TWAS MY OWN;

I MADE IT, FOR IT ONLY LIVED TO ME,

AND TO THE GOD WHO LOOKED INTO MY MIND.

THE PRELUDE - WILLIAM WORDSWORTH

Images of Nature | **ROMANTICISM**

Rosenblum in his book *Modern Painting and the Northern Romantic Tradition* was based on their need 'to revitalize the experience of divinity in a secular world that lay outside the sacred confines of traditional Christian iconography.'

Their works evoked for the first time an 'experience familiar to the spectator in the modern world, an experience in which the individual is pitted against, or confronted by, the overwhelming, incomprehensible immensity of the universe, as if the mysteries of religion had left the rituals of church and synagogue and had been relocated in the natural world.'

Ye presences of Nature, in the sky
Or on the earth! Ye visions of the hills!
And souls of lonely places! Can I think
A vulgar hope was yours when Ye employed
Such ministry, when ye through many a year
Haunting me thus among my boyish sports,
On caves and trees, upon the woods and hills,
Impressed upon all forms the characters
Of danger or desire; and thus did make
The surface of the universal earth
With triumph and delight, and hope and fear,
Work like a sea? THE PRELUDE – WILLIAM WORDSWORTH

The Romantic is aware of the immanence of the ideal in the real, the Heavenly Host as well as the golden guinea of fire when he sees the sun. Keats's *Ode to Autumn* and Shelley's *Autumn* suggest an inner essence of autumn as each conceives it whereas earlier writers concentrated on its outer manifestations.

The exception is the continuous tradition of visionary writers, the Celtic nature poets, for instance, but the Romantics allied the further notion of personality to nature.

The great achievement of Wordsworth was to relate nature to man's inner world of introspection. Transcendental feelings previously associated with religion were turned onto nature, and then incorporated into the psyche. Two hundred years later Wordsworth's view of nature, at least as expressed in his simpler poems, seems to have settled as our own – at least when we are on holiday.

Why were nature and landscape so important to the Romantics? The subject was not exactly new. Medieval lyrics, Chaucer, Shakespeare and even Milton are full of it, and in the eighteenth century when Pope's reputation was at its height, nature still makes many appearances.

So it is fair to say that the Romantic preoccupation with nature is a culmination of a trend begun in the eighteenth century with precursors long before that. Notable eighteenth-century writers on nature were James Thomson, Joseph Addison and William Collins. But there are differences which are considerable. Instead of observing and reporting what, say, a sunny spring morning looks and feels like, eighteenth-century poets such as Gray offer a muzzy personification.

The formula used by Wordsworth is equally applicable to visual artists: 'a selection of the language really used by men'. Romantic art and poetry aim at directly conveying the sounds, sights and scents of the world of nature. In the eighteenth century, nature and man are divorced.

Romantic art reflects a change of emphasis from a man-centred view of nature to that of an interaction between man and a natural world full of its own energies. Romantic artists respond to this world because it represents values of vital human importance, though embodied in non-human forms. In this internalisation of nature and its relation to feelings, they made nature into something new and exciting.

YE PRESENCES OF NATURE, IN THE SKY OR ON THE EARTH!
YE VISIONS OF THE HILLS!

THE PRELUDE – WILLIAM WORDSWORTH

A track pursuing, not untrod before,
From deep analogies by thought supplied
Of consciousness not to be subdued,
To every natural form, rock, fruit or flower
Even the loose stones that cover the highway,
I gave a moral life: I saw them feel,
Or linked them to some feeling… THE PRELUDE - WILLIAM WORDSWORTH

The Romantics moved from sheltered nature into the wild and perceived it for its own sake, not for projected meaning. The form and nature of poetry was changed by Wordsworth to reflect a truth that he felt existed in a natural state. As well as in his poetry, Wordsworth directly contributed to the new view of nature by writing the influential *Guide to the Lakes*. A story is told of Wordsworth towards the end of his life when a clergyman asked him if he had written any other books.

To begin, then, with the main outlines of the country; I know not how to give a
distinct image of these more readily, than by requesting him to place himself with
me, in imagination, upon some given point; let it be the top of either of the
mountains, Great Gavell, or Scawfell; or, rather, let us suppose our station to be
a cloud hanging midway between these two mountains, at not more than
half a mile's distance from the summit of each, and not many yards from their
highest elevation… GUIDE TO THE LAKES - WILLIAM WORDSWORTH

Nature for Wordsworth becomes spirit, source of simple pleasures, comforter, bridge between inner and outer worlds, the developer of the poetic mind, and source of morality.

So was it with me in my solitude;
So often among multitudes of men.
Unknown, unthought of, yet was I most rich –
I had a world about me – 'twas my own;
I made it, for it only lived to me,
And to the God who looked into my mind. THE PRELUDE - WILLIAM WORDSWORTH

Throughout nineteenth-century Europe, landscape and nature became major themes for artists and writers. In Germany Goethe was overwhelmingly influential. A vision of nature was created that began both to include elements of religion and to supersede it. Goethe wrote:

The revolution which I foresaw and which is now going on within me, is the one which has arisen in every artist who has long and zealously been loyal to Nature, and then seen the remnants of the great, ancient Spirit; his soul has welled up and he has felt a kind of inward transfiguration of himself…

GOETHE LETTER 30 SEPTEMBER 1786 QUOTED IN GOETHE'S DIARY

The results of this vision can be seen in many areas: the central importance of Die Externsteine rocks as a mystical centre of Germany; in Wagner's Gothic vision of nature; and in the revival of interest in the Grail, to be found through a sacred quest in landscape. In the new German cinema, the same feeling occasionally breaks through, for instance, in the films of Werner Herzog.

Running through American attitudes to landscape is an epic sense of space. This is a particularly blessed country, a landscape before the Fall, a paradise on earth. The huge size of the country, the notion of the frontier and the scale of colonization all contributed to this vision.

American art can be seen to have been dominated by this Romantic vision of landscape until the 1960s. Two central images thrown up by this landscape are that of the traveller, reliant first on the stagecoach and then on the car, and that of the west.

A TRACK PURSUING, NOT UNTROD BEFORE,
FROM DEEP ANALOGIES BY THOUGHT SUPPLIED
OF CONSCIOUSNESS NOT TO BE SUBDUED,
TO EVERY NATURAL FORM, ROCK, FRUIT OR FLOWER
EVEN THE LOOSE STONES THAT COVER THE HIGHWAY,
I GAVE A MORAL LIFE: I SAW THEM FEEL,
OR LINKED THEM TO SOME FEELING...

THE PRELUDE – WILLIAM WORDSWORTH

THE GUIDE, THE GUARDIAN OF MY HEART, AND SOUL OF ALL MY MORAL BEING.

Lines Written A Few Miles Above Tintern Abbey – William Wordsworth

BORROWDALE, Cumbria
One of the Lakes' most beautiful and dramatic landscapes

The beautiful Borrowdale valley runs north from the central fells of the Lake District, carrying the River Derwent into the lake of Derwent Water, a landscape well known to such lovers of the Lakes as John Ruskin and Beatrix Potter.

The valley contains several scenic villages and such spectacular features as Lodore Falls and the 'Jaws of Borrowdale', where the breadth of the valley is squeezed into a gorge.

BUTTERMERE, Cumbria
The spectacular view from Red Pike

The view of Buttermere from the summit of Red Pike is regarded by many to be one of the finest views in the Lake District. Along with High Crag and High Stile, Red Pike forms the trio of Buttermere Fells and gains its name from the syenite present in its rocks and subsoil, which give the fell its distinct reddish colouring.

Buttermere has various literary associations. Rosemary Sutcliff's novel *Shield Ring* is inspired by the semi-mythical figure of Jarl Buthar and his Cumbrian rebels and their last stand against invading forces after the Norman conquest.

Melvyn Bragg's *The Maid of Buttermere* is based around the life of Mary Robinson (1778–1837), who was the landlord's daughter at The Fish Inn in Buttermere village.

DERWENT WATER, Cumbria
The landscape of Beatrix Potter's childhood

Flanked by the Lake District towns of Keswick and Portinscale and surrounded by wooded fells, Derwent Water is one of Cumbria's most romantic and scenic lakes, popular with both walkers and sailors alike.

Some three miles long and one mile wide, the lake contains several islands, all under the care of the National Trust. Derwent Island was possibly first settled by copper miners in the 16th century, and in the 1770s the eccentric Joseph Pocklington built a house on the island and entertained the locals with spectacular firework displays and fake naval battles.

Stunning views of Derwent Water can be had from nearby Friars Crag – a view described by the art critic John Ruskin (1819–1900) as one of the three or four most beautiful views in Europe.

Beatrix Potter (1866–1943) also fell in love with the unspoilt beauty of the area while spending childhood holidays at Lingholm, a property by the lake, and she recorded the landscape in the nature sketches that would inform her famous children's books.

It was while staying near Ambleside, some miles to the south, that the Potter family met the Rev. Hardwicke Rawnsley, a man who would do much to help preserve Britain's historic buildings and landscapes as one of the founders of the National Trust.

In 1905 Potter bought Hill Top, a Lakeland farm near Hawkshead and now a National Trust property. She continued to acquire farms in the area, and, when she died in 1943, she left these and some 4,000 acres to the Trust to be preserved for posterity.

KENTMERE, Cumbria
A Lakeland valley rich in archaeological remains

The village of Kentmere lies north of the Windermere – Kendal road at the head of the Kent valley. The valley contains a particularly rich crop of prehistoric remains, including traces of a settlement of round huts at Tongue House in the northern part of the valley.

KIRKSTONE PASS, Cumbria
Wordsworth's 'savage pass'

...inaccessible high, rocky, barren hills, which hang over one's head in some places and appear very terrible
Celia Fiennes, 1698

The modern-day tourist finds romance and beauty in the scenery of the Lakes. This has not always been the case. In 1698, that intrepid traveller Celia Fiennes felt suitably uncomfortable as she journeyed from Kendal to Patterdale via Kirkstone Pass (on the present-day A592), at 454 metres the Lakes' highest road-pass. In the 1720s, Daniel Defoe thought the landscape "the wildest, most barren and the most frightful of any that I have passed over in England".

It was not until the publication in 1757 of Edmund Burke's aesthetic principles regarding the 'sublime and the beautiful' that ways of looking at landscape began to change. The very landscape that had so repelled Fiennes and Defoe could astonish and inspire as well as terrify

through its sheer grandeur and beauty, as evidenced by the works of the Lakeland Poets such as William Wordsworth and Samuel Taylor Coleridge.

Travel guides to the region, including Thomas West's *A Guide to the Lakes* (1778), popularised the area to such an extent that by the end of the 18th century it had become Britain's favourite tourist destination.

Even in 1807, crossing Kirkstone Pass was still an arduous business: the poet Thomas De Quincey recorded that the road was little more than a shepherd's track. The Pass is still a challenge for the modern motorist, with a 1 in 4 gradient in places. At the top lies the Kirkstone Pass Inn, the third highest pub in Britain.

PATTERDALE, Cumbria
Alfred Wainwright's favourite valley

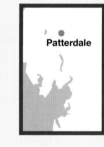

The Lakeland village of Patterdale lies at the southern end of Ullswater at the head of a valley that is one of the most popular with fell-walkers in the region – indeed that great walker Alfred Wainwright (1907–91) stated it was his favourite valley in the region, being relatively undisturbed by tourism.

The village is a favoured starting place for various walks, including the Striding Edge path to the summit of Helvellyn.

KIRKBY LONSDALE, Cumbria
'Ruskin's View', Turner and the Pre-Raphaelites

One of the loveliest views in England – JOHN RUSKIN

From behind St. Mary's Church in the historic Cumbrian market town of Kirkby Lonsdale, the visitor can look out over a curve of the River Lune towards the distant hills and enjoy what has become known as 'Ruskin's View'.

When the influential critic, social theorist and artist John Ruskin (1819–1900) saw the painting that his artistic hero, J. M. W. Turner, had made of this very spot, he was moved to remark: "I do not know in all my own country, still less in France or Italy, a place more naturally divine."

Ruskin urged artists to imitate Turner's example by seeking direct inspiration from nature, and thus to depict it truthfully rather than follow the 18th-century preference for idealised landscape painting.

In 1851, Ruskin controversially declared his support for the Pre-Raphaelite painters such as John Millais, William Holman Hunt and Dante Gabriel Rossetti, seeing in their precise and detailed observation of nature the embodiment of his aims for a new English art movement.

It was to be a stormy relationship, but in Ruskin these new young turks of British art had found a powerful, perceptive and influential champion.

RYDAL MOUNT, Cumbria
The heart of Wordsworth's Lake District

The poet William Wordsworth (1770–1850) was born, lived and died in the former Lake District county of Cumberland.

Although he also studied at Cambridge, travelled extensively on the Continent (including time spent in Revolutionary France) and lived for a spell near the poet Samuel Taylor Coleridge in Somerset, Wordsworth had an abiding love for the atmospheric landscape of the Lakes and it inspired some of his greatest poetry.

He was born in Cockermouth (his birthplace, Wordsworth House, can still be visited), was educated at Hawkshead Grammar School, and from 1799 to 1808 returned to the Lake District to live with his beloved sister Dorothy at Dove Cottage, Grasmere, until his growing family forced him to seek alternative accommodation.

Wordsworth needed the close companionship of his friends and family. He also needed the solitude required for creativity. He found both at Rydal Mount, the house near Ambleside that would be his home from 1813 until his death.

The house commands magnificent views over Lake Windermere, Rydal Water and the surrounding fells, and Wordsworth, a keen gardener, did much to landscape the property's four-acre garden to his own design. In a quiet corner of the garden he constructed his 'writing hut', which provided both shelter and privacy.

The house, which still belongs to the poet's descendants, contains Wordsworth family portraits, papers, personal possessions and first editions of the poet's works.

IN MY BEGINNING IS MY END. IN SUCCESSION
HOUSES RISE AND FALL, CRUMBLE, ARE EXTENDED,
ARE REMOVED, DESTROYED, RESTORED, OR IN THEIR PLACE
IS AN OPEN FIELD, OR A FACTORY, OR A BY-PASS...

EAST COKER, PART OF FOUR QUARTETS – T. S. ELIOT

Images of Nature | **TWENTIETH CENTURY**

With the advent of the Industrial Revolution, Romantic and other images of nature battled with industrial society, which was rapidly changing the face of the earth and thus creating the modern world.

In the process, new methods of perceiving the world and nature's ideological and complex role within it were developed by the revolutionary thinkers in the new social sciences.

In my beginning is my end. In succession
Houses rise and fall, crumble, are extended,
Are removed, destroyed, restored, or in their place
Is an open field, or a factory, or a by-pass…

EAST COKER, PART OF FOUR QUARTETS – T. S. ELIOT

By 1900 most of the wilderness no longer existed, at least in men's minds. The start of the twentieth century saw the municipalisation of the countryside and the beginning of planning on a national scale and its ownership greatly changed. Roads broke it up, traffic thundered through it. The idea of nature as a pantheistic spirit was no longer part of culture. Nature was available as a leisure pursuit at weekends and holiday time.

The First World War and consequent social and political changes produced countryside of greatly changed ownership. Control of land was increasingly in the hands of large public and private corporations. At the same time access to nature was greatly increased. More and more people were able to enjoy it.

Despite this greater social equality in relation to nature, artists and poets working with landscape fought what they considered to be a rearguard action. Writers such as D. H. Lawrence contrasted the country and the city. In 1922 T. S. Eliot created one of the central landscape images of the century – that of *The Waste Land* based on

Grail legend, but referring to the twentieth century and his vision of a barren material and psychological landscape of man.

Here is no water but only rock
Rock and no water and the sandy road
The road winding above among the mountains
Which are mountains of rock without water
If there were water we should stop and drink
Amongst the rock one cannot stop or think
Sweat is dry and feet are in the sand…

THE WASTE LAND - T. S. ELIOT

Marshall McLuhan thought that Eliot, influenced by Dante, Flaubert, Baudelaire and Joyce, was creating a psychological landscape.

Whereas in external landscape diverse things lie side by side, so in psychological landscape the juxtaposition of various things becomes a precise musical means of presenting, without the copula of logical enunciation, experiences which are united in existence but not in conceptual thought.

TENNYSON AND PICTURESQUE POETRY - MARSHALL MCLUHAN

Stanley Spencer worked at Cookham, Paul Nash in many disparate places. By 1950 educated holiday-makers had been taught to see most of the wilderness and views of Britain by artists and poets. Cornwall and other extreme margins of Britain became the chosen landscapes of landscape artists. The oldest inhabitants of Britain and contemporary artists choose the same places to live.

In the 1960s this mystical or romantic strand became the basis of the counter-culture. Rock groups such as Pink Floyd, often in 'natural' settings such as the Glastonbury Festival, invoked nature as an emblem of purity and renewal in opposition to the alienation of advanced technological society.

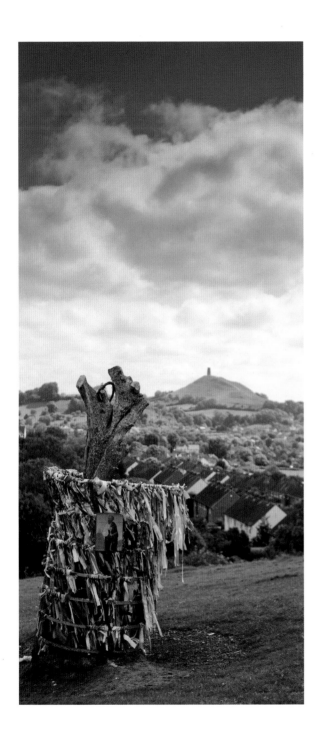

Whilst artists fought in isolation on the margins, popular culture was disseminating a view of nature derived from the picturesque and the Romantic poets.

An additional theme was controlled or planned images of nature. As population and accompanying industrialisation and urbanisation increased, so planning of the 'environment' became essential and inevitable. The early socialists pioneered the realisation that if the natural social and economic order was allowed to develop unchecked, then man lived a life that was terrible and against his nature – unless, that is, it is human nature to live in a slum and work eighteen hours a day.

The British expressionistic cinema of the 1930s and 1940s contained particularly compelling images of nature. Celia Johnson's and Trevor Howard's journey through idyllic scenes of Yorkshire countryside in his MG in *Brief Encounter* and the Scottish landscapes in *The 39 Steps* and *I Know Where I'm Going!* are especially evocative. These uniquely British cinematic images of nature provide a powerful relief for psychological conflict, internal turmoil and difficulties in relationships. A structure of external nature is being provided for feeling that offered a containment through these film images. In music Elgar, Vaughan Williams, Delius and Benjamin Britten composed powerful musical evocations of nature.

Behind many of the best twentieth-century projects were ideas of nature derived from landscape gardening. The landscaping of motorways, garden cities and new towns are particular examples. That these influences were not always powerful enough to overcome planning blight is also true.

In the twentieth century, landscape becomes the equivalent or starting point for many different directions. Of *Totes Meer (Dead Sea)* (1940) Paul Nash writes:

THE THING LOOKED TO ME SUDDENLY, LIKE A GREAT INUNDATING SEA.

OUTLINE - PAUL NASH

The thing looked to me, suddenly, like a great inundating sea. You might feel under certain influences, a moonlight night for instance, this is a vast tide moving across the fields, the breakers rearing up and crashing on the plain. And then, no: nothing moves, it is not water or even ice, it is something static and dead. It is metal piled up, wreckage. It is hundreds and hundreds of flying creatures which invaded these shores...By moonlight, this waning moon, one could swear they began to move and twist and turn as they did in the air. A sort of rigor mortis? No, they are quite dead and still. The only moving creature is the white owl flying low over the bodies of the other predatory creatures, raking the shadows for rats and voles.

Nash described his preoccupation:

The landscapes I have in mind are not part of the unseen world in a psychic sense, nor are they part of the Unconscious. They belong to the world that lies, visibly, about us. They are unseen merely because they are not perceived; only in that way can they be regarded as 'invisible'. OUTLINE - PAUL NASH

Every holidaymaker sent a picture postcard of a favourite view. Camping became a dominant holiday mode. Films used landscape as did popular fiction to represent a safer, more traditional world where urban life, class and pain were overcome by natural surroundings to create a dream world.

The New Town movement took the city into nature. The new towns were called 'garden cities'.

But unease about what was being done to nature remained and artists stayed on the margins, close to the Neolithic encampments. St Ives in Cornwall became a centre of a form of painting between landscape and abstraction. Landscape remained a strand in art, but it was no longer dominant. Henry Moore, however, wrote: 'It is this mixture of figure and landscape. It is what I try in my sculpture. It is a metaphor of the human relationship with the earth, with mountains and landscape.'

It is to Australia and America that the landscape tradition leads. Only in Land Art does nature become a main theme. In the culture as a whole, the back-to-nature movement had powerful support in the counter-culture of the 1960s and the ecological movement.

In our advanced industrial culture, eclecticism and co-existence are the order of the day, and contemporary views of nature vary from the behaviourist to the mystical. The city is so much more important than the country.

As man learned to separate himself from his potentially devouring Mother Earth, so the distinction between nature and culture increased. So much so that in our own day we feel it has gone too far. Yet, at the same time, the more comfortable man made himself, the more inclined he was to look at the fearful mother with a kindly eye – indeed even to idealise her.

But the haunting image of nature in the twentieth century is a starker one – the rejection of nature and sometimes even its actual destruction.

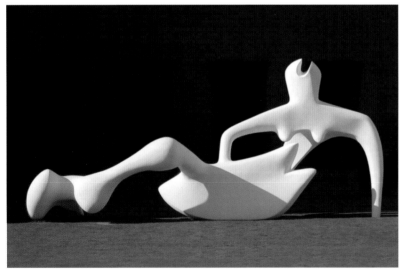

THERE'S NOT A MAN THAT LIVES WHO HATH NOT HAD HIS GOD-LIKE HOURS AND KNOWS WHAT MAJESTIC SWAY WE HAVE AS NATURAL BEINGS IN THE STRENGTH OF NATURE

THE PRELUDE – WILLIAM WORDSWORTH

HIS SENSITIVENESS TO MAGIC AND THE SINISTER BEAUTY OF MONSTERS WAS STIRRED

A LETTER - RUTH CLARK

THE PYRAMIDS OF MY SMALL WORLD, A BEAUTIFUL LEGENDARY COUNTRY
HAUNTED BY OLD GODS LONG FORGOTTEN

Outline – Paul Nash

IN MY BEGINNING IS MY END

THERE IS NOT EVEN SILENCE IN THE MOUNTAINS

BUT DRY, STERILE THUNDER WITHOUT RAIN

THERE IS NOT EVEN SOLITUDE IN THE MOUNTAINS

BUT RED SULLEN FACES SNEER AND SNARL

FROM DOORS OF MUDCRACKED HOUSES...

THE WASTE LAND - T. S. ELIOT

AVEBURY, Wiltshire
The inspiration for Paul Nash's Equivalents for the Megaliths

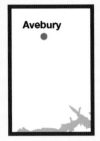

Avebury

"the hallowed remnants of an almost unknown civilisation"

In July 1933, the painter and critic Paul Nash (1889–1946) embarked on a journey that would have a profound impact on his art. His destination was the market town of Marlborough in Wiltshire, from which he travelled a few miles west to visit Avebury, site of the largest known stone circle in the world.

Jaded with having to undertake commercial commissions in order to earn a living, Nash was galvanised by the experience. *"If anything will preserve my interest in landscape from a painter's point of view,"* he wrote, *"it will be this country."*

Throughout his life, this most poetic of British landscape painters discovered his 'places' where nature and the ancient features of the landscape combined to weave a spell on his imagination. He found them in a wide, and often surprising, variety of locations – from a quiet corner of London's Kensington Gardens and the trenches of the First World War to the Sussex coast close to Rye and at Wittenham Clumps near Oxford.

At Avebury, Nash had discovered his 'landscape of the Megaliths'. As his friend, Ruth Clark, put it, *"his sensitiveness to magic and the sinister beauty of monsters was stirred"*.

This Wiltshire landscape spoke to Nash of Britain's ancient and mystical heritage as it did to other British landscape artists of the 20th century, such as Graham Sutherland, John Piper and Eric Ravilious. But Nash also responded to the abstract quality of Avebury, and in his unsettling 1935

landscape, *Equivalents for the Megaliths* (Tate Britain), he interprets the massive sarsen stones as cylindrical objects posed against the Wiltshire landscape.

Fundamentally even older than Stonehenge some 20 miles to the south, Avebury dates from around 2600 BC, its 27 remaining stones (of a possibly 97) arranged in a circle so vast that it encloses the village of Avebury, with its fine manor house and church.

Many find the Avebury stone circle even more impressive than Stonehenge, and with good reason. A processional avenue of stones leads up to the circle from the south and close by lies the extraordinary mound of Silbury Hill, which is similar to the 'ringed' hill seen in the distance in Nash's *Equivalents for the Megaliths*.

Visitors to Avebury may also be curious to see the nearby Sanctuary and the West Kennet Long Barrow, one of the largest, most impressive and most accessible Neolithic chambered tombs in Britain.

EAST COKER, Somerset
T. S. Eliot's family roots and final resting place

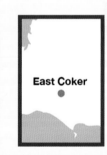

East Coker

"In my beginning is my end."
"In my end is my beginning."

These two lines drawn from the writings of the 14th-century mystic Julian of Norwich top and tail *East Coker*, one of four lengthy poems that comprise what many believe to be T. S. Eliot's (1888–1965) masterpiece, *Four Quartets*, which was instrumental in Eliot being awarded the Nobel Prize for Literature.

Eliot visited this Somerset village in 1937 and published *East Coker* three years later. East Coker represented for

Eliot an English idyll at the start of the Second World War, and the poem focuses on mankind's relationship to the passage of time and on life, death and the continuity between the two.

The four poems (*Burnt Norton, East Coker, The Dry Salvages* and *Little Gidding)* are all inspired by actual locations and events in Eliot's life and each represents one of the four elements – 'earth' in the case of *East Coker*.

East Coker in itself represents Eliot's beginning and end: his ancestors migrated to America from the village in the 1660s – one of them apparently serving on the jury of the notorious Salem Witch Trials – and his ashes are buried in the church.

SALISBURY PLAIN, Wiltshire
A vast and ancient landscape

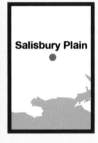

Here is the heart of our island: the Chilterns, the North Downs, the South Downs radiate from hence. The fibres of England unite in Wiltshire, and did we descend to worship her, here we should erect our national shrine

The Longest Journey – E. M. Forster

Writing about the view from the fictional Wiltshire hill-fort of Cadford Rings, E. M. Forster captured the essence of one of this country's most distinctive and archaeologically rich landscapes: the open expanse of Salisbury Plain.

We have the Army to thank for preserving the Plain much as it would have been in Forster's day and even further back into history. In the first half of the 20th century the Army bought up about half of the Plain's 300 square miles and it is still used as the UK's largest military training ground. Being sparsely populated and crossed by a few minor roads, much of the Plain remains as rolling, rugged grassland.

The precise boundaries of the Plain are difficult to define, but essentially it extends north to the Vale of Pewsey, west to Warminster and Westbury, east to Ludgershall and Tidworth (where the Plain extends over the county border into Hampshire) and south to the A303. Stand on the southerly reaches of the Plain and on a clear day you can just make out the spire of Salisbury Cathedral, the tallest in the country.

The Plain is famous for its wildlife and archaeology, and a vast number of Iron Age hill-forts are scattered around its boundaries – Bratton Camp near Westbury, with its spectacular views and sturdy White Horse, is well worth a visit.

Salisbury Plain provided inspiration to other writers besides E. M. Forster, including Thomas Hardy and William Wordsworth. In Hardy's *Tess of the d'Urbervilles*, the fugitive Tess and her husband, Angel, take refuge at the Plain's most famous monument, the 'heathen temple' of Stonehenge, long before it became a tourist mecca.

In the early 19th century, in their dramatic watercolours the artists John Constable and J. M. W. Turner captured the monument's 'sublime' qualities as well as its isolation within the Plain's wild but beautiful vastness.

WITTENHAM CLUMPS, Oxfordshire
Paul Nash and the landscape of Totes Meer (Dead Sea)

The thing looked to me, suddenly, like a great inundating sea. You might feel – under certain circumstances – a moonlight night for instance, this is a vast tide moving across the fields, the breakers rearing up and crashing on the plain. And then, no: nothing moves, it is not water or even ice, it is something static and dead. It is metal piled up, wreckage.

In August 1940, as part of his duties as a war artist, Paul Nash (1889–1946) visited a dump for wrecked military aircraft at Cowley on the south side of Oxford. Nash felt the place was haunted: "a pervasive force baffled yet malign hung in the heavy air." He made sketches and took photographs, and from this scene of devastation and destruction fashioned one of his most distinctive works:

Totes Meer (Dead Sea), now in the collection at Tate Britain.

Nash's eye transformed a mass of twisted metal into a turbulent but frozen seascape, over which hovered the moon and the disturbing white shape of an owl. This iconic masterpiece made a deep impression on Sir Kenneth Clark, the art critic and Chairman of the War Artists Advisory Committee. He pronounced it: "Most beautiful – the best war picture so far, I think."

An heir to the poetic, visionary art of William Blake, Samuel Palmer and the Pre-Raphaelites, Nash had a profound love of the British landscape and was acutely sensitive to the 'spirit of place'. Another location – not

that far from Cowley – that had a lifelong impact on his art was Wittenham Clumps, a pair of rounded, tree-topped hills about 10 miles south of Oxford, one of them a prehistoric hill-fort.

Nash called the Clumps "the Pyramids of my small world", "a beautiful legendary country haunted by old Gods long forgotten". Their distinctive silhouettes recur throughout his work, most notably in the late paintings *Landscape of the Summer Solstice* (1943) and *Landscape of the Vernal Equinox* (1944), in which Nash's habit of viewing the Clumps distantly through binoculars gives the landscape a peculiarly foreshortened appearance.

Wittenham Clumps remain popular with present-day visitors. One can climb the Clumps, look out over the panorama of the Thames Valley and enjoy the landscape around these two strange little hills. The view to the west was improved in 2014 by the demolition of the less-than-lovely cooling towers of Didcot Power Station.

ZENNOR, Cornwall
Patrick Heron, D. H. Lawrence and the West Cornish landscape

Zennor was the artist Patrick Heron's spiritual home. Born in Headingley, Leeds in 1920, Heron spent much of his childhood in west Cornwall and would never forget the light and colour of the landscape. In 1956 he returned to live in this 'sacred land' and moved into Eagle's Nest, a house overlooking the Atlantic at Zennor. He would live in this small village, which lies a few miles west of St. Ives on the twisting road to St. Just, until his death in 1999.

This move to the wild, almost lunar, landscape of this part of the Cornish peninsula, with its rough, hilly moorland strewn with massive rocks, had a profound impact on Heron's art, as did the Tate Gallery's landmark 1956 exhibition of the American Abstract Expressionists.

In 1958, Heron started to work in his friend Ben Nicholson's former studio in nearby Porthmeor and turned from figurative painting to abstraction. Influenced by the jagged lines of the coast and the granite boulders that dotted the surrounding countryside, he formulated his distinctive painting style of the 1960s and 1970s. Through the use of bold shapes and vibrant pigments, Heron sought to achieve a perfect balance between colour and space.

Patrick Heron is just one of the artists who have sought solace or inspiration from this remote landscape. The writer D. H. Lawrence – facing conscription and fearing a nervous collapse after the reception of his 'obscene' novel, *The Rainbow*, during the First World War – fled London with his wife, Frieda, and moved into a cottage just outside Zennor, where he worked on *Women in Love*. Fellow writers Katherine Mansfield and her husband, John Middleton Murry, joined them.

This arrangement ended when the damp weather took its toll on Mansfield's health and the Lawrences were wrongly accused by the locals of being spies (the German-born Frieda was related to the enemy air ace 'The Red Baron'). They left Cornwall abruptly, and after the War left Britain for good.

Other local places of interest include Zennor's church of St. Senara, which contains the famous 'Mermaid of Zennor' bench-end carving, and high on the windswept moorland stands Zennor Quoit, an imposing prehistoric burial chamber.

In Conclusion

In my beginning is my end. Now the light falls
Across the open field, leaving the deep lane
Shuttered with branches, dark in the afternoon,
Where you lean against a bank while a van passes,
And the deep lane insists on the direction
Into the village, in the electric heat
Hypnotised. In a warm haze the sultry light
Is absorbed, not refracted, by grey stone.
The dahlias sleep in the empty silence.
Wait for the early owl.

EAST COKER, PART OF FOUR QUARTETS – T. S. ELIOT

Different times emphasise different aspects of nature.

There's not a man
That lives who hath not had his god-like hours
And knows not what majestic sway we have
As natural beings in the strength of Nature.

THE PRELUDE – WILLIAM WORDSWORTH

Beneath the variety of concerns the portrayal of the land, and experience of the land, seems to correspond to a basic human need. At times this representation of the land has created visionary landscapes where heaven and earth combine. At other periods the need to dominate, plan or create distance from what we call nature has predominated. But even where this is so, in the history of attitudes to land and landscape in Britain, a great love of nature is apparent.

LIGHT FALLS ACROSS THE OPEN FIELD

East Coker, part of Four Quartets – T. S. Eliot

Indexes

Photographs © Adrian Munsey

Names and Places

Selected Bibliography

Brandt, Bill. *Literary Britain.* Aperture, 1986

Carus, Carl Gustav. *Nine Letters on Landscape Painting: Written in the Years 1815–1824 with a letter from Goethe by Way of Introduction.* Getty Publishing, 2003

Eliot, T. S. *Four Quartets.* Faber & Faber, 2001

Eliot, T. S. *The Waste Land and Other Poems.* Faber & Faber, 2002

Forster, E. M. *The Longest Journey.* Penguin Classics, 2006

Hardy, Thomas. *Tess of the d'Urbervilles.* Wordsworth Editions Ltd, 1992

Heron, Patrick. *The Colour of Colour.* University of Texas Press, 1979

Hoskins, W. H. *The Making of the English Landscape.* Little Toller Books, 2013

Hunt, John Dixon and Willis, Peter (eds). *The Genius of the Place: The English Landscape Garden 1620–1820.* MIT Press, 1988

Hunt, John Dixon. *The Figure in the Landscape: Poetry, Painting, and Gardening during the Eighteenth Century.* Johns Hopkins University Press, 1989

Jackson, Kenneth (ed.). *Celtic Miscellany.* Penguin Classics, 2006

Jackson, Kenneth. *Studies in Early Celtic Nature Poetry.* Cambridge University Press, 2011

Jung, Emma and von Franz, Marie-Louise. *The Grail Legend.* Princeton University Press, 1998

Lévi-Strauss, Claude. *The Savage Mind.* Weidenfeld and Nicholson, 1994

Long, Richard. *Walking the Line.* Thames & Hudson, 2005

Macfarlane, Robert. *The Old Ways: A Journey on Foot.* Penguin, 2013

Michell, John. *The New View Over Atlantis.* Thames & Hudson, 1986

Nash, Paul. *Outline.* Faber & Faber, 1949

Rosenblum, Robert. *Modern Painting and the Northern Romantic Tradition: Friedrich to Rothko.* Thames & Hudson, 1978

Schama, Simon. *Landscape and Memory.* Harper Perennial, 2004

Schlegel, A. W. *Vorlesungen über schöne Literatur und Kunst.* Nabu Press, 2012

Stone, Brian (tr.). *Sir Gawain and the Green Knight.* Penguin, 1974

Weston, Jesse. *From Ritual to Romance.* Creative Space Independent Publishing Platform, 2013

Williams, Raymond. *The Country and the City.* Spokesman Books, 2011

Wordsworth, William. *Guide to the Lakes.* General Books LLC, 2012

Wordsworth, William. *The Prelude: The Four Texts.* Penguin Classics, 1995